London Theatre

Frontispiece. Roy Dotrice as John Aubrey in *Brief Lives*, first staged at the
Hampstead Theatre Club, 16 January 1967.

London Theatre
from the Globe to the National

James Roose-Evans

PHAIDON · OXFORD

For My Mother
with love and gratitude

Acknowledgements

I should like to thank Mrs Foster and Miss Tracy of the British Theatre Centre's Reference Library for their patient and sympathetic assistance; Mrs Emma Dickinson; Suzanne O'Farrell of the Theatre Museum at the Victoria and Albert; the Garrick Club; my editor Pendleton Campbell who has shown remarkable patience, enthusiasm and faith in this book; and above all, J. C. Trewin, critic and scholar, who undertook the task of reading and correcting the manuscript and making a number of valuable comments which have been incorporated into the text.

Phaidon Press Limited, Littlegate House, St. Ebbe's Street, Oxford
First published 1977

ISBN 0 7148 1766 X
Filmset and printed in Great Britain by
BAS Printers Limited, Over Wallop, Hampshire

Contents

List of Illustrations

'As soon as there is, on four raised planks, no matter where, a man, and nothing round about him, expressing himself in the whole range of his means of expression, theatre will be there—and, if one likes to call it so, total theatre.'

JEAN-LOUIS BARRAULT

'A man walks across an empty space while someone else is watching him, and this is all that is needed for an act of theatre to be engaged.'

PETER BROOK

'A piece of theatre needs a space, an audience, some actors, imagination, and a leader.'

HELEN MIRREN

Introduction

The evolution of theatre in the western world may be seen mirrored in the history of the London theatre over the past four hundred years, from the founding of The Theatre in 1576, the first public playhouse in London, to the opening of the National Theatre in 1976. Within the boundaries of one city, over those four centuries, every form of theatre can be found, from street theatre with processions, displays, stage-booths and fairs, to elaborate spectacles at Covent Garden, and experimental stagings in countless public houses, upper rooms and basements.

In this book I have attempted to trace the different stages in the evolution of theatre in London, as well as of some of its theatres, and to show how the buildings reflected the personalities of those who worked in them, and of the audiences who filled them. Above all, in so far as space has permitted, I have tried to relate my story to the changing social conditions of each period.

I am not a scholar—one who writes out of a life-time's research of a particular subject—but a working director. My approach to this book has been that of a theatre director researching the background of a particular period play. The director always has to know more than his actors, not in order to deliver a series of seminars, but so that, out of a wealth of detail, he may be able to kindle their imaginations. Too much detail and an actor, like the ordinary reader, can be swamped.

In rehearsing a period play it is detail that can bring alive both the text and a sense of period. Macready, writing to a friend, concerning the part of Kitely in the Elizabethan play, *Every Man In His Humour,* enumerates certain props and details of business which the friend, who is playing the part in an amateur production, might consider using, and then adds the significant remark, 'I could turn that to account.'

The research for this book has led me into strange labyrinths and backstreets of London, brought me many meetings and encounters, and into areas that have been destroyed beyond recall, as well as before locked doors to which no keys have yet been found. But, emerging from this journey into the past, I hope that I have been able to turn to account for the ordinary reader something of the endless fascination of the many people who have made London theatre. As Martha Graham has said, 'Theatre is an act before it was a place,' and that act can occur anywhere. There is conscious drama—the craft, the profession—and there is unconscious drama, which each one of us enacts from moment to moment. One cannot have theatre without this sense of drama. Barbara Hepworth used to describe how, seated in St Mark's Square, Venice, she loved to watch the tourists emerging from the narrow side streets into the huge open space of the piazza, and to observe how each person physically confronted the challenge of that space, whether striding boldly into its centre, or keeping shyly to the sides. She was the conscious spectator watching the unconscious protagonist upon the stage of St Mark's Square, and in the theatre the spectator is watching the conscious performance of the actor, whether it be a dancer entering the huge space of the Covent Garden stage, or an actor, such as Roy Dotrice as John Aubrey in Patrick Garland's memorable production of *Brief Lives,* alone in a room crowded with books and antiquities, suddenly aware of the audience, like a single visitor, to whom he begins to gossip about the past.

Gossip is an essential in the telling of history. Dates, bare facts and lists, necessary to scholarship, are like the bricks that provide the structure, but it is the details of gossip about people that furnish the house, and create its ambience. The stories about Lilian Baylis and the Old Vic are countless. It is the richness of her personality that haunts the building and has made it a much loved theatre.

A book is of value only in so far as it leads one on, to another book, or to another experience, opening up new areas. There is no special skill in constructing such a book as this, the fascination stems from history itself, from the diaries of Samuel Pepys or James Boaden, from the achievements of actors such as Macready and Phelps, of managers like Elliston or George Alexander, or of determined fanatics like the carpenter John Potter, who built the Little Theatre in the Hay, or Lilian Baylis, determined that her locals across the river should have the experience of Shakespeare.

Many have died without seeing their work bear fruit. The more one knows of history, the more one learns to acquire a long perspective, learning to think not in terms of one lifetime but of many generations. In 1848 one man conceived the idea of a national theatre for England and it was to be more than a century before it was realized. As King Arthur says in *The Quest for the Holy Grail*: 'for this is the purpose for which God sent you to us: to consummate what others have had to renounce, and to bring to conclusion all those things that no other was ever able to resolve.'

One constant factor remains throughout this story, the presence of the river Thames, which flows, as a living symbol, constantly changing and adumbrating with meaning, through this story of London's theatre. In Elizabethan times its waters were clear, and salmon could be fished from it; in Victorian times it received the filth of sewers emptied into it; for centuries it was a highway for traffic and commerce. Its character is constantly changing and so, in the same way, there can be no neat and tidy conclusion to this story, with the image of the National Theatre, four hundred years after the building of the first public theatre in London, rising, phoenix-like, from its ashes. In the remaining years of this century the forms of theatre will go on changing, and the new National Theatre is like one of those sets of Chinese boxes, each containing one within the other. The Cottesloe Theatre, at the National, is such a box, an empty space, and it may well be that from this smallest theatre in Denys Lasdun's mighty fortress will erupt the most powerful of these changes. Or it may come from quite an unexpected quarter. Theatre is, of its very nature, subversive, unpredictable, wasteful, generous, dangerous—an organic process. To quote from that scholar of theatre, actor, playwright, director, Harley Granville Barker, a man whose influence is out of all proportion to the actual number of plays he directed, 'There never was, and there never will be, an ideal theatre. The theatre is too complex and too delicate a machine, depending on the harmonious co-operation of too many talents and influences ever to reach perfection for more than a passing moment. The very greatest theatres at their greatest periods have been severely criticized, not, as a rule, without reason.'

London 1976

Chapter one

1567—1642

great noises·little eyases·Caterpillars of a Commonwealth

'England in 1558 was a backward country . . . not simply in comparison with its conditions today, but backward even when compared with some other countries of the sixteenth century. Beggary walked abroad in the land . . . essentials became scarce, prices rose, and by the middle of the sixteenth century the government faced with bewilderment and dismay the full blast of a runaway inflation, until then without parallel in English history . . . .

'London was the centre of politics, of administration, of religion, of law, of commerce. It was the social centre for the leading men of the age, with their great houses along the Thames. It was a great cultural centre with its Inns of Court; its theatres; its Chapel Royal. It was a pioneer in social welfare, with its Christ's Hospital, dealing with the care and education of poor children; St Bartholomew's for the sick, St Mary Bethlehem (Bedlam) for the mentally sick; it had its Bridewell workhouse, and its system of local taxation to pay for this and much else. All this was consolidated on a national scale in the great statutes of 1598. But London remained a great slum, overcrowded, poverty-stricken, diseased, which, like a giant mantis spider, killed off many thousands of those who were drawn in fascination towards her.'

JOEL HURSTFIELD

Shakespeare's London was still a medieval city, enclosed within its many gated walls. At Ludgate, the nearest entrance to the river, prisoners could be heard begging alms through the gratings of the gaol. There were five prisons in the city: the Cage, Cripplegate, Fleet, Newgate, and Ludgate, while across the river, in Southwark, were five more: the Clink, Compter, Marshalsea, King's Bench and White Lion. From Ludgate the wall went northward to Newgate, which for centuries had served as the main entrance to the city. Newgate was to survive until 1881, reserved for the worst class of offenders, herded together regardless of sex, age or offence, in conditions that, even in the nineteenth century, were a byword for overcrowding and filth. From Newgate the wall continued northward to Aldersgate, thence to Cripplegate and Moorgate, the latter created in 1415 for the use of carts and wagons from the country bearing timber and hay, and on to

Bishopsgate and finally Aldgate, where Chaucer once lived and wrote. From Aldgate the wall turned towards the Tower of London, which stood, moated and walled in, a town unto itself.

From these seven gates of London flowed a maze of narrow, darkened streets; dirty, smelling of bad drainage, but bustling with life. Carts and coaches thundered past, scattering the crowds. 'At every corner, men, women and children meet in such shoals that posts are set up of purpose to strengthen the houses, lest with jostling one another they should shoulder them down.' Porters sweating under their burdens, gallants newly arrived in town jangling their spurs, bright-eyed lawyers on the make, and soldiers returned from the wars, mingled with hawkers, colliers, apple-sellers, milk men, fishmongers, tinkers, and chapmen selling ribbons, lace and ballads. Apprentices, idling at street corners, would break into fights until the Sheriff's men appeared to make the peace. The opening scenes of *Romeo and Juliet* are as easily imaginable in Elizabethan London as in Renaissance Verona.

Entertainment was everywhere. Truly might Shakespeare write, 'All the world's a stage and all the men and women merely players.' Hanging was a regular spectacle, whether at Tyburn where thieves and murderers dangled, before being neatly disembowelled, their guts held up to the cheering crowds; or, at Execution Dock, below Wapping Old Stairs in Limehouse, where pirates were trussed up at low tide and the water rose above them. Thieves, their ears nailed to the pillory, would be provided with a knife with which to cut themselves loose, watched by enthusiastic audiences. Vagabonds would be tied to whipping-posts or dragged from the end of a boat across the Thames. Bawds were whipped through the streets, cheered on by lusty apprentices; while from the spikes of Bridgegate at London Bridge, heads of traitors leered like lop-sided flowers.

All along the riverside could be heard the watermen's cry of 'Eastward Ho!, and 'Westward Ho!, as they ferried passengers across the busy Thames crowded with ships and swans. 'From Greenwich to London it is a magnificent sight to see the number of ships and boats which lie in anchor, in as much that for two leagues you see nothing but ships that serve as well for war as traffic,' observed the French ambassador in 1597, while in 1544, the Spanish ambassador, enthusing about the Thames with its fine bridge crowded with houses, wrote, 'It is not possible in my opinion that a more beautiful river should exist in the world; for the city stands on each side of it, and innumerable boats, vessels, and other craft, are seen moving on the stream . . . . Never did I see a river so thickly covered with swans as this.' Was it of the Thames that Shakespeare was thinking when the Chorus in *Henry V* says:

> 'O do but think
> You stand upon the rivage and behold
> A city on the inconstant billows dancing;
> For so appears this fleet majestical . . .'?

In the long history of London's theatre, the river Thames runs like a glittering thread, from The Globe to The National.

On civic occasions, processions would blazon forth into the streets, a thousand men in armour, followed by morris-dancers, and white bears in carts. Similarly, pageants and processions would bring an added drama to the river, as companies of Guilds sailed in their gilded barges to escort a new Lord Mayor to Westminster, or welcome the Queen in her state barge. Decorated with banners and streamers, erupting with fireworks, heralded by drums and trumpets, the barges, many of them bearing elaborate tableaux, would glide past the crowded and cheering banks as all London (a city of 100,000 inhabitants) turned out to greet its monarch.

A great deal of entertainment was to be found in London, and Londoners were accustomed to going outside the city to tournaments at Smithfield, to the archery butts at Newington, to various athletic sports at Finsbury Fields and Shoreditch, while at Paris Garden the royal bulls, bears and mastiffs were kept caged, and baited in public, when not required across the river at Westminster or Whitehall. So popular were the bear-pits and bull-rings, so rowdy their audiences, that the phrase 'like a bear garden' has become immortalized in the English language and for at least three centuries was often enough an apt description of a theatre audience in London. Bear-baiting was not to be made illegal until 1835, while cock-fighting, though illegal, has once more appeared in England in the 1970s.

The annual fairs abounded with acrobats and tumblers, freaks and contortionists, jugglers and puppet shows. The puppets would be presented in temporary booths, at the fairs, at inns, or set up on street corners. Until well into the next century the puppet shows (or 'motions' as they were called) did much to preserve folk lore and Bible stories, the most popular being *The Creation of the World, Jonah and the Whale,* and *The Destruction of Jerusalem.* These folk plays were often topical, absorbing such contemporary events, as, for example, the Gunpowder Plot. The Elizabethan puppets were one of many popular forms of theatre in the London of the 1600s and 1700s, and patronized by all classes:

> To see a strange outlandish Fowl,
> A quaint Baboon, an Ape, an Owl
> A dancing Bear, a Giant's bone,
> A Foolish Engine move alone,
> A Morris dance, a Puppet play,
> Mad Tom to sing a Roundelay,
> A Woman dancing on a Rope,
> Bull-baiting also at the Hope,
> A Rhymer's Jests, a Juggler's Cheats,
> A Tumbler showing cunning feats,
> Or Players acting on the Stage—
> There goes the Bounty of our Age.

England has seen a long tradition of theatre, from the earliest miracle and mystery plays until the present day, when London theatre has become one of the tourist attractions of the world. Early in the sixteenth century, plays were performed by the Children of St Paul's, the choir school, while the boys' companies, 'the little eyases,' proved so popular that they became serious rivals to the companies of professional actors. At the Universities, amateur dramatic societies flourished, as well as at the Inns of Court.

The professional players staged their productions in the open air on trestle stages, or in the great halls of private houses. In London they flourished in the inn yards situated on, or off, Gracious Street (now Grace Church Street). When the plays were being performed, the streets would be even more crowded than usual and, since the plays were usually staged on Sundays and feast-days, they aroused the strong disapproval of the City Fathers and of the Church. Plays, thundered the Puritan preachers from their lofty pulpits, were the nest of the devil and the sink of all sin. The Lord Mayor continually complained to the Privy Council that the plays kept apprentices away from their work, as well as increasing the danger of infection in times of plague, encouraged thieving and whoring, and exposed audiences to the dangers of 'falling scaffolds, frames, stages, engines, weapons and powder used in plays.'

Protected as the players were, however, by their sovereign, Queen Elizabeth, the Lord Mayor and the City Fathers never quite succeeded in getting rid of the players, but they did succeed in hedging them round with so many prohibitions that in the end most of the companies found it easier to stay in the suburbs, outside the City walls, and just out of reach of the jurisdiction of the City.

By the middle of the sixteenth century, plays had gained such an extraordinary popularity that it is not surprising that, in 1567, an enterprising man called John Brayne, the rich brother-in-law of James Burbage the actor, decided to put up the money to convert an inn, the Red Lion in Shoreditch, into a theatre. A stage and seating were installed and this was the first permanent building to provide regular performances of plays. It was such a success that, in 1576—when William Shakespeare was twelve years old—Brayne financed a new project, devised by James Burbage, a member of the Earl of Leicester's Company of Players, to erect the first public playhouse to be built in London for use by a company of professional players. It was named The Theatre, and was in Shoreditch. We know very little about its structure and appearance. Any imaginary reconstruction is based mainly on our knowledge of its successors. Although we have the details of more than twenty companies of actors who worked in London during the Elizabethan and Jacobean period, we still have little actual knowledge of the stage craft used or even the kind of stage on which the actors played.

The Elizabethan Theatre, taking its precedent from the Cornish rounds, cockpits and tournament arenas, would appear to have been either polygonal or round in shape; hence the appropriateness of the name chosen for the first playhouse, taken from the word *amphi-theatre*. The originality of James Burbage's scheme lay in the simple device of an enclosure which enabled him to charge for admission.

The actual stage used by the players would, at first, have been identical with that used by all companies of strolling players for centuries, whether in the inn yards, on a village green, or in a banqueting hall—a platform set up on trestles, with curtains at the back to provide a tiring room where the actors could change, and from which they could make their entrances.

When Burbage built his theatre it was very much a gamble whether it would succeed and therefore the stage had to be mobile since the central yard was also used for a variety of 'activities,' from tumbling, dancing, vaulting, to fencing matches and exhibitions in the art of defence. It was probably a circular yard, some sixty feet in diameter, surrounded by three galleries each about ten feet high and twelve feet deep. In the lowest were 'standings' for the groundlings, and in the upper galleries three or four rows for those who could afford to pay more. On one side was the wall of the tiring house and, jutting out from it into the middle of the yard, the stage. At first the audience was not admitted into the yard, which was used as part of the acting area. On either side of the tiring house, as can be seen in the famous drawing of The Swan by de Witt, was a door—the prototype of the apron-stage doors of the Restoration theatre. At the back of the stage was an alcove, or inner stage, closed in with curtains. Above this was a balcony, flanked by two windows. In the de Witt drawing it is shown as being used either by spectators or, possibly, actors watching a rehearsal, but we know that it was often used as an acting area. Above this there might be another balcony. A roof was built over at least part of the stage, and this canopy, supported on pillars, was known as The Heavens. On its underside were painted the signs of the Zodiac. It is easy to see how Shakespeare was able to ally the physical qualities of the playhouse to the situation of a scene as in Hamlet's:

'Indeed it goes so heavily with my disposition, that this goodly frame, the earth, seems to me a sterile promontory: this most excellent canopy, the air, look you, this brave o'er-hanging firmament, this majestical roof fretted with golden fire . . . .'

Above the canopy was a hut which housed the machinery which raised and lowered, through a trapdoor, the various heavenly chariots, cloud-wreathed thrones or, as in *Cymbeline,* Jupiter in thunder and lightning sitting on an eagle. The thunder and other effects were also controlled from the hut.

As other theatres came to be built, and as they prospered, so they increased in splendour. They learned as they built, each new playhouse benefiting from the experience of the one that went before it. Visitors to these subsequent theatres were much impressed by the wooden columns 'which, painted like marble, could deceive the most expert.' The inside of the theatres would have been as colourful as any circus or fairground booth, fluttering with banners and flags, and musicians playing in the upper gallery. De Witt, visiting London about 1598, observed, 'There are in London four theatres of noteworthy beauty . . . in them a different action is daily presented to the people. The two first are situated to the southward beyond the Thames, named . . . The Rose, and The Swan . . . . Of all the theatres, however, the largest and most distinguished is . . . The Swan, since it has space for 3,000 persons and is built of a concrete of flint stones, and supported by wooden columns, painted in such excellent imitation of marble that it might deceive even the most prying.'

The Elizabethan, like the modern Roman, seems to have liked noise. Paul Hentzner, a German visitor, observed that the English were 'vastly fond of great noises that fill the ear, such as the firing of cannon, drums and the ringing of bells.' The theatres also used gunfire on every possible occasion, and the cannons would be fired just outside the theatres. Indeed, when there was a battle scene going on during a play at The Globe, on Bankside, the sound of the trumpets, the booming of the guns, and the shouting, could be heard on the other side of the river. In Ben Johnson's *The Silent Woman*, Morose, who cannot abide noise, names among the penances he would be willing to undergo for her, 'London Bridge, Paris Gate, Billingsgate, when the noises are at their height and loudest. Nay, I would sit out a play that were nothing but fights at sea, drum, trumpet and target.'

The Elizabethans also had quite a taste for realistic death scenes, for tortures and mutilations on stage. The actor would carry a hidden bladder of pig's blood which would spout when pricked by dagger or rapier. They also used animals' entrails for display as was done in reality with human entrails by the executioner at Tyburn. In the 1970s animals' entrails were used in the Grand Magic Circus production of *Robinson Crusoe,* when Man Friday tore out the innards of a dead man.

Each theatre carried a resident dramatist. At The Theatre it was Robert Wilson. Sometimes playwrights worked together, writing one act apiece, a method that was employed in Germany in the twentieth century by Erwin Piscator.

John Russell Brown has pointed out one crucial difference between the Elizabethans and twentieth-century actors—they actually ran their own theatres. They were not hired by the month or the year, nor were they under contract to any management. Ten or so actors would own the theatre, choose the plays, pay the dramatists, and take the profits. They acted in the plays with the help of 'hired men'—as the non-permanent actors were called—and boy actors who played all the female roles. They worked a repertory system so that, around the year 1600, one company might have thirty plays in production. We know that a single company in 1594 put on fifteen entirely new plays within six months, as well as revivals.

That first playhouse, The Theatre, was such an immediate success that in the following year Burbage built another next door, called The Curtain. This, too, prospered. Shortly afterwards, in 1587, a rival company, run by Philip Henslowe, opened a third playhouse over on Bankside, called The Rose. It is mainly thanks to the detailed records and account books kept by Henslowe that we know as much as we do. His leading actor was Edward Alleyn, the rival to Richard Burbage, the other great actor of the Elizabethan stage. Alleyn retired early, a wealthy man, from the stage, and founded the College of God's Gift at Dulwich whose boys ever since have called themselves Alleynians. It was from this college, in the twentieth century, that the National Youth Theatre was to make its first appearance.

The Theatre, The Curtain and The Rose, were the principal theatres that Shakespeare would have known when he came to London from Stratford-on-Avon, probably in the 1580s. Eventually, in the space of a single generation, from the latter half of the reign of Elizabeth I, until the Civil War in 1642, there were in London no fewer than fourteen theatres, nine of which were open to the public.

The two worst enemies of the players were the plague and the Puritans. Fortunately there was no severe outbreak of plague in the critical years that followed the opening of the first two public playhouses, although in 1577 they were closed in August and September for fear of spreading infection and the London companies had to go on tour.

The year 1577 also saw the publication of John Northbrooke's *Treatise Against Dicing, Dancing, Plays and Interludes*, in which the public's preference for plays to sermons provoked the preacher's worst reproaches. Stephen Gosson's *The School of Abuse,* published in 1579, contained 'a pleasant invective against Poets, Pipers, Players, Jesters, and such like Caterpillars of a Commonwealth.' This literature and the many virulent attacks that followed paved the way for action by the City Council of London. Either shortly before or after 1582 the Corporation decided to ban all performances of plays in the City and to petition the Privy Council for similar action in the suburbs. In 1584 the City requested the Privy Council to pull down The Theatre and The Curtain. Very surprisingly this request was granted. For reasons which we can only surmise—possibly through the intervention of the Lord Chamberlain on behalf of his own company of players who performed at The Theatre—the order was not carried out. Performances, however,were inhibited frequently and for long periods during this and the next decade as a result of outbreaks of the plague: Court and City acted as one in condemning public assemblies whenever the number of deaths ascribed to the plague began to rise sharply.

In the summer of 1592 severe plague hit London and raged, with some abatement in the winter months, until the summer of 1594. At the beginning of October 1592, the Lord Mayor's Feast was cancelled and the Michaelmas Law Term postponed. There was no question of reopening the theatres and the companies took to the roads. In January 1593 the plague deaths mounted afresh, and on 28 January the Privy Council inhibited 'all plays, baiting of bears, bulls, bowling and other like occasions to assemble any number of people together (preaching and Divine Service excepted).' At least 11,000 people died of the plague in 1593, the year in which the young dramatist Christopher Marlowe was stabbed to death in a brawl.

Most of the players, rather than face another ruinous exile in the country, hung about for some time in the hope that the outbreak would subside. There was an easing of the plague during Christmas 1593, but it gathered fresh momentum in February 1594 before finally burning itself out. Surfeited at last by its 20,000 victims, a fifth of London's population, the plague lay dormant. But it was followed by dearth and famine. The summer of 1594 was cold and wet, and those of the following two years little better, so that the green corn 'rotted ere his youth attained a beard, and the fold stood empty in the drowned field.' Those who had escaped death by plague at home and by battle abroad, were now threatened with starvation:

> Adieu, farewell earth's bliss;
> This world uncertain is.
> Fond are life's lustful joys—
> Death proves them all but toys:
> None from his darts can fly.
> I am sick, I must die—
> Lord, have mercy on us.

As Professor Halliday observes in *Shakespeare and His Age*, to have heard these words from Thomas Nashe's *The Song of the Plague*, sung by a boy to a lute, must have had, at that time, a peculiar poignancy. It is probable that Shakespeare wrote his death-laden tale of *Romeo and Juliet* during these two years of the plague. The play's final scene takes on a haunting reverberation in the light of this knowledge, as does so much of Shakespeare's writing:

> All lovers young, all lovers must,
> Consign to thee and come to dust.

In the June of 1594, the reorganized Chamberlain's Men assembled at The Theatre, where they were welcomed with open arms by old James Burbage and his eldest son, Cuthbert.

It was in 1596, the year Shakespeare's only son, Hamnet, aged eleven, died . . .

> He's all my exercise, my mirth, my matter;
> Now my sworn friend, and then my enemy;
> My parasite, my soldier, statesman; all:
> He makes a July's day short as December,
> And with his varying childness, cures in me
> Thoughts that would thick my blood . . .

that James Burbage bought the Parliament Chamber at Blackfriars for £600. Earlier, in 1577, Nicholas Farrant, producer of the Company of Boy Players of the Chapel Royal, Windsor, had rented part of Blackfriars for performances by various companies of choir boys. He had been very successful and attracted a better class of playgoer. James Burbage spent several hundred pounds in converting the interior of the Parliament Chamber into a theatre sixty feet long by forty-six feet wide, with two galleries. However, when the conversion was complete, the local residents (then as now) protested and got up a petition, claiming that their amenities would be destroyed. As a result the theatre remained empty until 1600, when it was rented by Henry Evans for the Children of the Chapel Royal. Patronized by the nobility and the gentry, the young actors were allowed by the residents and they flourished until 1608, when the company was dissolved by King James I for presenting plays that were too full of topical and personal allusions.

In 1596 The Theatre found itself threatened with a rival on the south bank. Some years before, Francis Langley, a London goldsmith, had bought the Manor of the Paris Garden, at the west end of Bankside and, soon after the reopening of the theatres in 1594, had decided to build a playhouse of his own, to be called The Swan. The London corporation protested, but Lord Burghley refused to intervene, Langley prepared to build, and Henslowe proceeded to make improvements to The Rose so that it might compete with the projected Swan theatre and its new devices.

It was probably about this time that the groundlings were let into the yard for the first time and nobles allowed to purchase stools on the stage itself. The yard was no longer an essential part of the playing area, whereas the revenue from the groundlings was—those groundlings whom Thomas Dekker described as 'stinkards glued together in crowds with the steams of hot breath.'

In 1597, the last year of the twenty-one-year lease of The Theatre, James Burbage died, leaving the building to his sons Richard and Cuthbert. The brothers asked the landlord, Giles Allen, to renew the lease of the land on which the building stood, but he, hoping perhaps to evade the issue, did not reply. In response, the two Burbages, together with William Shakespeare and their other partners, took the law into their own hands. They rented another plot of land over on Bankside and engaged a builder called Peter Street to pull down The Theatre and reconstruct it on the new site. The reconstruction of the old Theatre opened in the autumn of 1598 and was named The Globe Theatre, the most famous of all London's theatres and the scene of most of Shakespeare's greatest plays, in which Richard Burbage created many of the leading roles.

The building of The Globe was an expensive enterprise and in order to help pay for their new theatre The Chamberlain's Men sold a number of plays in the course of 1600. In August of that year *Much Ado About Nothing* and *Henry IV, Part Two* were registered together by two reputable publishers as 'Written by Master Shakespeare'—the first appearance of his name in the Stationers' Register, and soon afterwards the quartos appeared on the bookstalls.

Henslowe watched uneasily as the fine new playhouse went up opposite The Rose and when it was finished his worst fears were realized. Londoners flocked to see the plays of the now celebrated William Shakespeare being performed on the stage of the handsome new theatre, leaving The Rose half empty. Henslowe consulted with Alleyn, who was now his son-in-law. Alleyn, who had retired three years previously, agreed to come out of retirement, especially since the Queen had expressed the wish that he would act once more, and so he and Henslowe decided to build a new theatre in Finsbury, on the north bank of the river, within easy reach of the Inns of Court.

On 2 December 1599, a plot of land was leased and Henslowe contracted with Peter Street, the builder who had constructed The Globe, to build an even more handsome theatre which was to make their fortunes and to be called, appropriately, The Fortune. With Edward Alleyn as their leading man, the Admiral's Men opened at the new theatre in the autumn of 1600. Thus, at the turn of the century, the Chamberlain's Men had moved from Shoreditch to Bankside, and driven the Admiral's Men from Bankside to Finsbury. The Theatre and The Rose had been superseded by The Globe and The Fortune.

With the death of Queen Elizabeth in 1603 the theatres were once again closed and her funeral coincided with a fresh outbreak of the plague in which 30,000 died and which did not end until the spring of 1604. James I and his wife Anne were hurriedly crowned in Westminster Abbey, and all who could fled the capital. Nevertheless James found time for theatrical matters and only a week after his arrival in London he issued Letters Patent appointing The Chamberlain's Men as The King's Men, and the actors were duly sworn in as Grooms of the Chamber. Before the end of 1603, Edward Alleyn and The Admiral's Men were taken under the patronage of Prince Henry and became The Prince's Men, while Thomas Heywood and Worcester's Men were taken under the patronage of Queen Anne and became The Queen's Men. All three companies were authorized to play anywhere within the realm so that they were no longer subject to mayors and magistrates but became privileged members of the royal household. Almost by a single stroke the three leading companies were snatched out of the hands of their enemies while their Letters Patent, by specifying the places in which the Royal Companies were authorized to perform in London, served also to protect the players in their performances and their property. The actors and dramatists, however, as royal servants, could hardly avoid, albeit unconsciously, adapting their plays to the tastes of their royal patrons rather than of the more popular audience.

In 1613, during a performance of Shakespeare's play about Henry VIII, then called *All Is True,* The Globe Theatre was burned down when cannon were fired for the entrance of Henry VIII, and sparks accidentally ignited the roof thatch. Thomas Lorkin, writing to Sir Thomas Puckering, described how 'No longer since than yesterday while Burbage and his company were acting at The Globe the play of Henry VIII, and there shooting of certain chambers [small cannon or mortars] in way of triumph, the fire catched,' while John Chamberlaine, writing to Sir Ralph Winwood, 'But the burning of the Globe, on the Bankside, on St Peter's Day, cannot escape you; which fell out by a peal of chambers, the tampin or stopple of one of them lighting in the thatch that covered the house, burned it to the ground in less than two hours, with a dwelling house adjoining: and it was a great marvel and fair grace of God that the people had so little harm, having but two narrow doors to get out of.' Sir Henry Wotton, writing to his nephew a few days later, 'Now to let matters of state sleep, I will entertain you at present with what has happened this week at the Bank's side. The King's Players had a new play called *All Is True,* representing some principal pieces of the reign of Henry VIII, which was set forth with many extraordinary circumstances of pomp and majesty. . . . Now King Henry making a masque at the Cardinal Wolsey's house, and certain cannons being shot off at his entry, some of the paper or other stuff, wherewith one of them was stopped, did light on the thatch, where being thought at first but an idle smoke, and their eyes more attentive to the show, it kindled inwardly and ran round like a train, consuming within less than an hour the whole house to the very grounds. . . . Yet nothing did perish but wood and straw, and a few forsaken cloaks: only one man had his breeches set on fire, that would perhaps have broiled him, if he had not had by the benefit of a provident wit to put it out with a bottle of ale.'

When The Globe burned down, Henslowe proceeded to convert the Bear Garden into a regular playhouse, doubtless with the object of profiting by the misfortunes of his rivals. A certain edge of rivalry, of competition, is always necessary in the theatre. Henslowe went into partnership with Jacob Meade, a waterman, and the new theatre was to be called The Hope. A strong company came to play under the joint management of Henslowe and Meade, called The Princess Elizabeth's Servants, and one of the plays acted by them was Ben Johnson's *Bartholomew Fair,* the prologue of which is full of allusions to the new playhouse.

That Meade, a waterman, should have gone into partnership with Henslowe, offers an intriguing insight into the importance of the river Thames in this early history of London Theatre. It was in the interests of the watermen in general to increase the attractions of the Bankside. The Company of Watermen, in 1613, when The Globe was destroyed, fearful lest their business should suffer, had petitioned His Majesty 'that the players should not be permitted to have a playhouse in London or in Middlesex within four miles of the city on that side of the Thames'. Subsequently, John Taylor, the Water Poet, published a pamphlet justifying this petition, under the title, *True Cause of the Watermen's Suit Concerning Players and the Reasons that their Playing on London side is their* [i.e. the Watermen's] *extreme Hindrance,* in which he states that the theatres on the Bankside in Southwark were once so numerous, and the custom of going thither by water so general, that many thousand watermen were supported by it.

The majority, if not all, of those watermen had been sailors. In his Petitions to the Council, Taylor refers to their services abroad during Queen Elizabeth's reign, in the expedition to Portugal with the Earl of Sussex in the Armada Invasion, in the voyages of Sir Francis Drake, Sir John Hawkins, Sir Martin Frobisher, and others in Cadiz, in Ireland, in the Low Countries. These were the men who, from Whitehall to the Placentia at Greenwich, plied their trade as watermen, mixing freely with the sailors at the mouth of the Thames.

The Globe Theatre was rebuilt in 1614 and audiences once again piled in to see the plays while Henslowe saw his business dwindle, this time at The Hope, which became once more a bear garden—thus it is styled in Visscher's map of 1616. The Globe itself functioned until 1644 when, with the end of the lease, and the old theatres out of fashion, and the Puritans in power, it was finally pulled down.

The year 1609 was a turning point in the history of London theatre for it was then that Richard Burbage moved his company into The Blackfriars Theatre. The King's Men now had a private theatre which they could use as an alternative to the public Globe in the winter months. They were the first company of professional players to perform regularly indoors under conditions similar to those in the Great Chamber at Whitehall.

At the turn of the century, Bankside had been the centre of the theatrical world and The Curtain the only playhouse open on the north bank; but all this was reversed and The Globe became the only permanent theatre on the south bank. The Rose and The Swan became the scene for acrobats, fencers and prize-fighters, while The Hope, as we have seen, reverted to its original function as a bear garden. During the years 1616–23 it was to the private theatres in the neighbourhood of the Inns of Court that polite society began to flock, to Blackfriars and The Cockpit, while plans were afoot for building the Salisbury Court Theatre close to the abandoned Whitefriars.

The more intimate surroundings and the more select audience undoubtedly influenced the style of writing and playing. A standing audience is more volatile than a seated one, and it is one thing to declaim to an audience of two thousand people eating fruit, smoking tobacco, gossiping, and quite another to play before an intimate, sophisticated company of some two hundred educated men. Eventually The Blackfriars Theatre proved so successful (The King's Men were also able to charge higher prices to these more exclusive audiences) that the residents once again found it necessary to protest; coaches and crowds so congested the streets and the approach up Ludgate Hill, that they could not gain easy access to their houses. This time, however, the petition was not successful and Blackfriars continued to draw the town until the closure of the theatres in 1642. In 1616, the year of Shakespeare's death, The Cockpit in Drury Lane was roofed and converted into a private theatre for Queen Anne's Men.

When James I came to the throne in 1603, Shakespeare was an established playwright but he now had a rival, Ben Jonson, who was chiefly responsible for the return to fashion of the court masque—a hybrid entertainment which combined music–ballet–dance–poetry–drama and elaborate staging. These masques were expensive, extravagant, 'one-off' performances for the entertainment of the royal family and courtiers who often took part. Under James I they took on a new lease of life, and many thousands of pounds would be expended upon a single performance. From 1611, for nearly forty years, not a winter passed at Whitehall Palace without one or more of these elaborate entertainments, whose influence can be seen in Shakespeare's later plays—*Cymbeline, The Tempest*.

For these masques, Inigo Jones created the designs and decorations, and framed the whole within a proscenium arch in the Italian manner. *The Masque of Blackness*, for example, was presented in the old wooden banqueting house at Whitehall, at the lower end of which Inigo Jones set up a stage on wheels, forty feet square and four feet high. Under the stage was the machinery for the effects and framing it a Renaissance proscenium with a curtain to conceal the change of scenery. That evening's entertainment cost probably more than Queen Elizabeth had spent on masques in the whole of her reign. The extravagant masques with which Ben Jonson and Inigo Jones delighted the Court resulted gradually in a corruption of their taste for plays and the demand for spectacle began slowly to spread to the public theatres.

On 2 September 1642, a few days after the military operations of the Great Rebellion had commenced, parliament issued the 'First Ordinance Against Stage Plays and Interludes,' which ordered that 'public stage plays shall cease to be foreborne.' The remaining theatres were pulled down and it was decreed that 'players shall be taken as rogues.' The actors, however, as has happened in other countries and at other times under similar circumstances, went 'underground' and continued to perform surreptitiously.

Chapter two

1660—1685

the woman plays today· orange nymphs· Punch· fop's alley

During the eighteen years from 1642 to 1660 the theatre was rigorously suppressed. The Puritans also banned bear- and bull-baiting, morris-dancing, and ordered that all may-poles, which had long been a source of irritation to them, should come down. The Puritans were, above all, opposed to theatre in general and actors in particular; the latter were often whipped or fined and thrown into prison, as were the spectators who were bold enough to attend these illegal performances. To bypass parliament an actor called Robert Cox invented a form of entertainment, which combined music, dancing, mime and short comedy sketches, known as Drolleries. There is a print of Cox in *Simpleton the Smith* performing suggestively with a long French loaf. Cox's publisher wrote 'I have frequently known several of the female spectators "to long for it".'

In 1654 the authorities were so alarmed at the continuing frequency of the performances that, during the February of that year, instructions were given for 'the supressing of a wicked sort of people called Actors, and Plays. . . .' During that year, plays were so regularly staged at the Red Bull Inn (the playhouse where Pepys loved to go as a boy, and where Thomas Killigrew got free admission, along with other small boys, for impersonating pocket-sized devils) that troops would raid the inn in the middle of a performance and carry off the actors to the nearest magistrate. Throughout this period, however, the puppet plays continued unhindered.

In 1660 Charles II was restored to his throne. Bonfires were lit on the hillsides, wine ran in the streets, and the maypoles were set up once again. The theatre also was restored. Among his first acts on returning to England, the King granted Patents to Thomas Killigrew and Sir William D'Avenant to form two separate companies of players. Killigrew's was known as The King's Company and D'Avenant's as The Duke's Company, it being under the patronage of the King's younger brother, the Duke of York. During the reign of Charles I, D'Avenant had succeeded Ben Jonson as Poet Laureate, and was appointed Governor of the King and Queen's Company at The Cockpit Theatre. With the outbreak of the Civil War, both he and Thomas Killigrew had fled to France, remaining in exile with Charles II. They, like their sovereign, were great womanizers, and were among his boon companions. D'Avenant, we know, lost his nose from syphilis. John Evelyn records in his diary, 'He got a terrible clap of a black handsome wench that lay in Acre Yard, Westminster.'

The King had an intelligent taste for drama and was an avid theatregoer throughout his reign. He became a familiar and popular figure in his capital. He liked walking about with his spaniels, even taking them to the theatre, talking with chance acquaintances, gossiping with Fellows of the Royal Society, encouraging playwrights, discussing a new coin, or a new parterre in the royal gardens.

In 1660 Killigrew converted a tennis court in Vere Street, Clare Market, into a theatre, while he prepared to build a new theatre in Drury Lane. To Vere Street, in December 1660, audiences flocked to see a performance of *The Moor of Venice* (Shakespeare's play adapted) with a special prologue written by Thomas Jordan:

> I come unknown to any of the rest
> To tell you news : I saw the lady drest.
> The woman plays today, mistake me not,
> No man in gown or page in petticoat.

Until then, women's parts on the London stage had been played by boys. At this performance the part of Desdemona was played by Mrs Margaret Hughes, who thereby became the first English actress on the professional stage. Killigrew from then on used women in female roles, but D'Avenant continued to use female impersonators, even though some of them, as one critic remarked, had 'grown out of use like cracked organ pipes and have faces as old as our flags.' Killigrew, however, was so carried away that in 1664 he was to mount a play, *The Parson's Wedding,* with an entire female cast.

One of the most successful female impersonators was Edward Kynaston, who managed to hold his own alongside the women then crowding the stage. His skills so fascinated the ladies of quality that he would be collected from the theatre after a performance, still in his female costume, and driven about in their open carriages through Hyde Park for all to see. Since not enough women could be found and trained for the stage immediately, Edward Kynaston, James Nokes and others, were able to continue in D'Avenant's company. They also varied their repertoires by playing male roles as well, especially as they got older. Pepys records a visit to a performance of Ben Jonson's *The Silent Woman* in which Kynaston starred. 'He appeared first as a poor woman in ordinary cloth dress . . . then in fine clothes as a gallant, and in them was clearly the prettiest woman in the house; and lastly, as a man: and then, likewise, he did appear the handsomest man in the house.' From Pepys, a great womanizer, this was indeed high praise. Another contemporary playgoer also observed, 'It has since been disputable among the judicious whether any woman that succeeded Kynaston so sensibly touched the audience as he.'

In December 1661 there was a crowded house at Lincoln's Inn Fields for a performance of *Hamlet* with a new young actor, Thomas Betterton. Colley Cibber's account of this provides a vivid glimpse of a playhouse at this period. 'The audience indifferent enough in the opening scenes. The fine gentlemen laugh loudly and comb their periwigs in the "best rooms". The fops stand erect in the boxes to show how folly looks in clean linen, and the orange nymphs . . . giggle and chatter as they stand on the benches below with young and old admirers, proud of being recognized in the boxes.

'The whole court of Denmark is before them but, not till the words, "Tis not alone my inky cloak, good mother", fall from the lips of Betterton is the general ear charmed . . . then, indeed, the vainest fops look round and listen too . . . The voice is so low and sad and sweet, the modulation so tender, the dignity so natural, the grace so consummate, that all yield themselves silently to the delicious enchantment. "It's beyond imagination!" whispers Mr Pepys to his neighbour, who only answers with a long drawn, Hush!

'. . . And now, as Hamlet's first soliloquy closes, and the charmed but silent audience "feel music's pulse in all their arteries", Mr Pepys almost too loudly exclaims in his ecstasy, "It's the best acted part ever done by man." And the audience think so too; there is a hurricane of applause, after which the fine gentlemen renew their prattle with the fine ladies, and the orange girls beset the Sir Foplings.'

Whenever we read in the chronicles of the seventeenth-century theatre that the audience was silent, it is almost invariably an indication either of the magnetism of a great actor such as Betterton or Garrick, or of the beauty of a Nell Gwyn. The noise of a Restoration playhouse was often intolerable. Betterton once complained that the voices of the spectators 'put the very players out of countenance.' Not that the other actors were any better. 'On the stage,' wrote Betterton in his *History of the English Stage,* 'not only the Supernumeraries as they call them, or Attendants, seem regardless of the great Concern of the scene, and even the Actors themselves who are on the Stage, and not in the very Principal Parts, will be whispering to one another, or bowing to their Friends in the Pit, or gazing about.'

On 8 May 1662, Samuel Pepys visited Covent Garden to look at a picture hanging in an alehouse, and went 'thence to see an Italian puppet play that is within the rails there, which is very pretty, the best that ever I saw and great resort of gallants.' Later that year, this same puppet theatre performed before the King at Whitehall. Everywhere it went, it became noted for its chief character, Pollicinella, which finally was shortened to Punch. The stage built in Whitehall for Signor Bologna's marionettes measured twenty feet by eighteen. From now on the old Elizabethan glove puppet was driven to the background, not to reappear until towards the end of the eighteenth century. Puppets began to find their way into the nursery, where Punch became a great favourite, as we learn from a letter by Sir Thomas Browne in 1682. The theatres in which the marionettes were presented at the fairs would have been booth-theatres. Just before the end of the seventeenth century, Joseph Addison, in 1698, wrote a poem describing a typical booth-theatre at a London fair:

> From far and near, the gay and curious come,
> Enter the booth and fill the spacious room:
> Not undistinguished are the honours there,
> But different seats their different prices bear.
> At length, when now the curtain mounts on high,
> The narrow scenes are opened to the eye. . . .
> All actions that on life's great stage appear
> In miniature are represented here.
> But one there is that lords it over all,
> Whom we call Punch, or Punchanello call,
> A noisy wretch, like boatswains always hoarse,
> In language scurrilous, in manners coarse.

In 1663 Thomas Killigrew moved to his new theatre in Drury Lane, The King's House, or Theatre Royal. The Vere Street Theatre was subsequently used as a Nursery, or training school for young actors, by both Killigrew and D'Avenant (the latter eventually started his own Nursery in Hatton Garden) until 1671. From 1675 to 1682 it was used as a Nonconformist Meeting House, later becoming a carpenter's shop, then a slaughter-house, and finally destroyed by fire in 1809.

Sir William D'Avenant's company played first at the Salisbury Court Theatre in Fleet Street, and afterwards in Portugal Row, then in Lincoln's Inn Fields.

The King's House in Drury Lane (The first of the four theatres to be built on this site) was constructed almost entirely of wood. There were no stalls in the Restoration theatre and the floor of the house was occupied mainly by the pit with its backless benches covered with matting. In rainy weather the glazed cupola over the pit let in rain or hail. Killigrew opened this theatre to the public on 7 May 1663 with *The Humorous Lieutenant* by Beaumont and Fletcher, and Ann Marshall played the part of Celia. She was therefore the first woman to act on the stage of Drury Lane. When the play was revived in 1666 the role was taken over by a new actress, Nell Gwyn.

It was shortly after the opening of the King's House that Nell Gwyn obtained a job there as an orange girl. It is likely that she got it through Mrs Mary Moggs, more commonly known as Orange Moll. She was in charge of the orange girls who paraded the pit with baskets of oranges and other fruit. Mrs Moggs was a widow who knew all the gossip of the theatre: which actress or which orange girl was sleeping with which nobleman. Pepys mentions her several times for she often carried messages for him from his actress friend Mrs Knipp when the latter wanted an assignation. Orange Moll lived in the parish of St Paul's, Covent Garden. On one occasion, when a gentleman in the audience had been guzzling his oranges with undue haste and appeared to be choking to death, Orange Moll forcibly thrust the obstruction down his throat, in the middle of a performance. She held a licence to sell not only oranges but lemons, fruit, sweetmeat and nuts. The presence of these women in the theatre was to last into the nineteenth century. Clement Scott described a visit at the age of eight to Drury Lane in 1849, and the chatter of monotonous cries from the orange women, dragging their heavy baskets through the pit benches: 'Oranges, apples, ginger beer, bills of the play!'

Nell Gwyn's beauty was so striking, however, that she was not destined to remain an orange girl for long. After eighteen months she became an actress and by 1665 she appeared to be on the threshold of a dazzling theatrical career when, once again, the plague struck London. Six years later she retired to become the King's mistress for sixteen years.

At the King's Theatre, no seats were reserved. The moment the doors opened at midday, people pushed their way in and sat on a bench until the play started at about 3.30 p.m., unless they had paid a boy, or sent a servant, to keep a place for them. There was also a curious system, which persisted well into the eighteenth century, whereby the management permitted any member of the audience to see the first act free of charge; if, after that, they wished to stay on, they then had to pay. Quite an art developed, especially among the younger, for dodging the doorkeeper after the first act and so staying on to see the rest of the entertainment without paying: a time-honoured custom, for even in the 1960s it was possible to slip in to see the Royal Shakespeare Company at the Aldwych Theatre in London through a special door, known to a few, and obtain a free seat in the gallery just as the house lights were going down.

Audiences were noisy. The orange girls would haggle loudly over prices and fights would break out at the slightest provocation. One April evening in 1682, at the Dorset Gardens Theatre, a quarrel broke out between Charles Dering and a Mr Vaughan, which led to the two drawing their swords and, since there was not enough room in the crowded pit, they climbed onto the stage and fought there.

Pepys, who was a snob, preferred the theatre when lords were present. He often complained when 'the house was full of citizens,' but very often royal visitors were little more refined in their manners. Early in January 1663, the Duke of York and his wife honoured a play of Killigrew's by their presence and Pepys records, 'they did show some impertinent and methought unnatural dalliances there, before the whole world, such as kissing of hands and leaning upon one another.' Nell Gwyn is seen gossiping with Pepys, who is ecstatic at this attention, or she is glimpsed lying across the laps of three young beaux in order to converse with a fourth. The patronage of the Court and of the nobility increased the popularity of the drama, while the common knowledge that Charles II had made mistresses of actresses in both Killigrew's and D'Avenant's companies encouraged his courtiers and the young bloods to follow suit.

If one of the beaux failed to find what he was looking for among the prostitutes or orange girls, and grew tired of parading his finery on the apron stage—which became known as Fops' Alley—he could pay to go backstage and chat up the actresses in their dressing-rooms. Here they would comment with such coarseness on what they saw or, teasingly, were not allowed to see, that the more modest actresses would dismiss their young dressers. When they had completed their make-up and were clothed, they would dismiss the young beaux who then wandered back into the auditorium to talk loudly with the orange girls, occasionally turning to listen to the dialogue on stage, or to bandy exchanges with some masked lady in a box. In those days, before the vizard fell into disrepute, ladies would appear, unattended, in masks, in the boxes. The battle of wits between them and the beaux was often so much more amusing than what might be passing on the stage that the audience nearby would listen to them rather than to the actors. To this end Pepys once took his place in 'the upper bench next the boxes' and described it as having 'the advantage of seeing and hearing the great people.' Emily Dickinson once wrote:

> The show is not the show,
> But they that go.
> Menagerie to me
> My neighbour be.
> Fair play—
> Both went to see.

Certainly in the London theatre of the seventeenth and early eighteenth centuries, audiences went as much to view one another as the actors. Lord Foppington in 1697 did not pretend to be a beau but he remarked, 'A man must endeavour to look wholesome lest he make so nauseous a figure in the side box that the ladies should be compelled to turn their eyes upon the play.' Constantly the ladies in the boxes would be subjected to the intentionally audible criticisms of 'the little cockerels of the pit,' with whom the more daring would engage in repartee. Later in the century we read that the beaux would run from one playhouse to another 'and, if they like neither the play nor the women, they seldom stay any longer than the combing of their periwigs, or a whisper or two with friends, and then they cock their caps and out they strut again,' their eyebrows and periwigs redolent with the essence of orange and jasmine. The perfume was probably necessary for the habits of the English were as dirty as the streets of London through which flowed rivers of filth, there being no attempt at a proper system of drainage until late in the century. The periwig of William Fanshaw stank so much that Nell Gwyn begged him to buy himself a new one so that 'she might not smell him stink two storeys high when he knocks at the outward door,' while Mrs Pepys records that she once found in her husband's hair 'twenty lice, little and great.'

Prostitutes thronged the London theatres. Time and again, in his prologues,

Dryden attacked the ill-manners of the beaux and the flagrant behaviour of the prostitutes:

> The Playhouse is their place of Traffick, where
> Nightly they sit, to sell their Rotten Ware:
> Though done in silence, and without a crier,
> He that bids the most is still the buyer;
> For while he nibbles at her amorous train,
> She gets the money but he gets the clap.
> Intrencht in vizor they giggling sit,
> And throw deigning looks across the Pit,
> Neglecting wholly what the actors say,
> Tis their least business there to see the play.

For seventeen years London had been remarkably free from the plague. In 1665 it returned. Pepys, abroad in Drury Lane on 7 June of that year, observed two or three houses with a red cross on the doors, and three days prior to this the Lord Chamberlain had ordered the theatres to be closed because of the plague. They were not to be open again until October 1666. Now the city suffered a final onslaught of dreadful intensity. Week after week the death toll mounted. By the end of June there was a mass exodus from the city. The King and Government fled to Oxford. Nearly 70,000 people died in London alone. For those like Pepys who were compelled to remain in the city it was a time of horror. At night it was no longer the sedan chairs being carried through the streets by liveried servants, with link boys, holding torches of tow and pitch, going ahead and shouting, 'Make way for my Lord!', but the tolling bell of the death cart and the repeated cry of 'Bring out your dead!'

By late March 1666 Pepys was longing for the theatres to reopen, 'but God knows when they will begin to act again.' He went to see the alterations to the stage that Killigrew was planning at the King's House, Drury Lane. 'My business here was to see the inside of the stage and all the tiring-rooms and machines; and indeed it was a sight worth seeing. But to see their clothes, and the various sorts, and what a mixture of things there was; here a wooden leg, there a ruff, here a hobby-horse, there a crown, would make a man split himself to see, with laughing; and particularly Lacy's wardrobe and Shotrell's. But then again to think how fine they show on the stage by candlelight and how poor things they are to look at near to hand, is not pleasant at all.'

In September of that year occurred another catastrophe, the Great Fire of London, which destroyed a large part of medieval London. The fire broke out on the night of 1 September 1666 in Pudding Lane. Most of the houses were built of wood. The river was crowded with boats carrying the furniture and belongings of those able to flee to the waterside. To the watchers, the sky itself appeared to be on fire. When it was over, the King, with Christopher Wren, planned the rebuilding of London. Visitors to London at this time found it a beautiful city but were appalled by its smell and by its dirt. Prince Cosimo III of Tuscany, visiting England in 1669, was enchanted by the 10,000 small boats on the Thames, which plied their trade between Windsor and the Fleet, or ferried passengers from one bank to another, but he took objection to the slops emptied from upper windows, and the pigs that wandered the littered streets. The plague itself, across the centuries, had been carried by rats which infested London like other cities. Public houses were numerous in London at this time and beer was drunk in large quantities. Coffee houses also were fashionable. There was one in particular, in Bow Street, Covent Garden, frequented by the literary personalities of the day. Here John Dryden, poet and dramatist, had a special chair reserved for him by the fire in winter, and on the balcony in summer.

1670 saw the first performance of Buckingham's play *The Rehearsal*, in which Dryden, who had succeeded to the post of Poet Laureate when D'Avenant died in 1668, was the chief target of Buckingham's wit. John Lacy, who took the part of Bayes, the hapless playwright conducting rehearsals of his latest tragedy, faithfully imitated Dryden's mannerisms to the delight of audiences at Drury Lane.

One year later, however, the King's House was destroyed by fire. 'A fire at the King's playhouse between 7 and 8 p.m. on Thursday evening last,' (25 January 1672), wrote an eyewitness, 'which half-burned down the house and all their scenes and wardrobe: and all the houses from the Rose Tavern in Russell Street on that side of the way to Drury Lane are burned and blown up, with many in Vinegar Yard: £20,000 damage. The fire began under the stairs where Orange Moll keeps her fruit. Bell, the player, was blown up.'.

Until a new theatre could be built the company had to make do at Lisle's Tennis Court. D'Avenant's old company had opened two months previously at the magnificently decorated Dorset Garden Theatre. D'Avenant's widow, and later his son Charles, in collaboration with Thomas Betterton, continued to attract large audiences with spectacular operas, which included Sir William's version of *Macbeth* (with singing witches), and Shadwell's operatic version of *The Tempest*. The Duke's Company prospered.

A new theatre in Drury Lane was not ready until March 1674. Designed by Sir Christopher Wren, it held about 1,260 spectators, an intimate, square-shaped auditorium. In April 1682 it was forced to close its doors and the two companies merged. On 16 November the United Company, as it was called, opened a season at the Theatre Royal, Drury Lane. The theatre in Dorset Square was only occasionally used and from 1682 to 1695 there was only one theatre in London.

The period between 1659 and 1700 was one in which many of these authors set out to improve Shakespeare. D'Avenant took *Measure for Measure* and *Much Ado About Nothing*, and combined them into a comedy entitled *The law Against Lovers*. Dryden rearranged *Troilus and Cressida*, and joined with D'Avenant in destroying

The Tempest. Nahum Tate, the Poet Laureate, but remembered now solely fo. travesties of Shakespeare, metamorphosed *Richard III* into *The Sicilian Usurper*, while *Coriolanus* became *The Ingratitude of a Commonwealth.* Tate also altered *King Lear*, cutting out the character of the Fool, making Edgar and Cordelia lovers. The climax of the play showed the King and his daughter, hand in hand, alive and happy ever after. 'In my humble opinion,' wrote Addison, 'it has lost half its beauty.' Yet Tate's version of *King Lear* was to hold the stage for many years.

In the London theatre, the regular use of scenery did not take place until 1664. When the Duke's Company opened at Lincoln's Inn Fields in 1661 with D'Avenant's opera, *The Siege of Rhodes,* there was a somewhat crude version of the picture-frame stage. The platform stage and proscenium doors, a notable feature of English theatres, were to persist into the twentieth century. As Allardyce Nicoll has remarked, 'On the Continent the whole of the original Olympic "proscenium" was moved forward to the front of the stage; in England, it remained for a century and a half at the rear of the actors'. Although in 1775 Drury Lane was redesigned by the Adam brothers, its apron stage projected about thirteen feet into the auditorium. In his early years, David Garrick would act his big scenes well forward on this appron with the audience around him, rather than behind the picture-frame of the proscenium arch; until 1765, light came from seventy-two candles in six large chandeliers above his head—which also illuminated the auditorium throughout the performance— and from a row of footlights. Pepys had occasion to refer to the heat from these candles, likening the atmosphere of the auditorium to a furnace.

In February 1667 he records a conversation with Thomas Killigrew. 'He tells me that the stage is now by his pains a thousand times better and more glorious than here-to-before. Now, wax candles, and many of them; then, not above three pounds of tallow; now, all things civil, no rudeness anywhere; then, as in a bear garden; then, two or three fiddlers; now, nine or ten of the best; then, nothing but rushes upon the ground, and everything else mean; now, all otherwise.'

Considering the rowdy behaviour of audiences it is hardly surprising that the players preferred to act downstage on the apron, while the scenery beyond the proscenium arch provided a distant and decorative background. Instinctively the actors knew that in order to be heard and in some measure control their audiences they had to be as close to them as possible. New theatres, experimenting with the relationship of audience and players, might have been attempted but for the restricting effect of the exclusive right given to the two patented theatres, a restriction that was to dog the history of London theatre for over a hundred and fifty years. The Restoration, while it restored the freedom to act, by no means permitted the unrestricted, and organic, growth of privately owned public theatres which had been possible in Shakespeare's day.

The death of Charles II in 1685 had profound effects upon the royal theatre.

Where the players had been guaranteed an enlightened ear for their troubles, and a tolerance for anything that seemed at all risqué, the advent of William III in the Glorious Revolution of 1688 meant that they, like everyone else, had to toe the line. William's Queen Mary was genuinely pious, and her successor Queen Anne, was even more a champion of public decorum.

The end of the century saw the London theatre in decline. Congreve's *The Way of the World* failed to bring it additional lustre. Dancers, strong men, tumblers, horses, were called in to attract the crowds. The public greeted these with greater enthusiasm than poets. King William cared more for the feats of Kentish strongmen than for the plays of Shakespeare. Just as the Restoration of Charles II had seen a reaction against Puritan values, so the coarseness of the intervening years provoked a change in moral tone. There was a resurgence of Puritanism which lasted until the coming of Wesley. The moral code of the aristocracy was, slowly, being replaced by that of the upper middle-class in an increasingly mercantile society.

Chapter three

The Eighteenth Century : I

puppets·Patent Theatres·pantomime·The Guards on stage

In the first decades of the eighteenth century, London was a small but growing city. Theatrically, however, it was limited. The old Tudor playhouses on Bankside were gone, as were The Cockpit, The Red Bull, The Blackfriars, and The Salisbury Square theatres; while the great theatre in Dorset Garden, conceived by William D'Avenant and built by Christopher Wren, was derelict and out of action. From having a number of theatres, London now had only two.

Only two new theatres were officially built after the establishment, in 1663, of The Theatre Royal at Drury Lane. One of these was Covent Garden in 1732, and the other was The King's House in the Haymarket, built in 1705 by Sir John Vanbrugh. This theatre was a source of trouble from the start. Built under a special licence from William III it was far too grandiose in design for, as Colley Cibber observed, what could those vast columns, 'their gilded cornices, their immoderate high roofs avail, when scarce one word in ten could be heard distinctly in it? . . . this extraordinary and superflous space occasioned such an undulation from the voice of every actor that generally what they said sounded like the gabbling of so many people in the lofty aisles of a cathedral!' The actors soon returned to act in Lincoln's Inn Fields, and it became instead the established home of Italian opera. Most of Handel's operas and nearly all his early oratorios were first performed there. In 1720 a Royal Academy of Music was founded there and Handel was engaged to write a series of operas. Like the South Sea Bubble of the same period, the scheme exploded. The theatre itself was destroyed by fire in 1789, rebuilt in 1790, when its interior was then the largest in England, capable of holding 3,000 people. It was again burned down in 1867, rebuilt and in 1875 became, for a time, a centre for the singing envangelists, Moody and Sankey. In 1891 this theatre was demolished and the fourth, and present, theatre (Her Majesty's) opened in 1899.

In 1720, across the street from The King's House, a carpenter named John Potter, without a licence and without consulting anyone, built The Litttle Theatre in the Hay (eventually to be known as The Theatre Royal, Haymarket). One of the first people to establish a success at this small theatre was the novelist and dramatist Henry Fielding when, in 1730, he staged there his play, *The Author's Farce,* in which he satirized the craze for Italian opera, poked fun at the way audiences ran after new attractions, such as acrobats, tumblers and marionettes, at the expense of the legitimate drama. He followed this success with another, *Tom Thumb,* in which, as Vanbrugh had done before him in *The Rehearsal,* and Sheridan in *The Critic,* he ridiculed the mannerisms of the stage of his day, especially the rhetorical ranting style of acting

The marionette theatres were, in fact, miniature theatres, and the eighteenth century was their heyday as a form of entertainment. In 1707, at Bartholomew Fair, in Mrs Mynn's booth, Elkanah Settle presented *The Siege of Troy,* which had taken ten months to prepare. In one scene the Trojan Horse appeared, seventeen feet high, out of which emerged forty soldiers in full armour; in another scene, through the use of gauzes, lights and highlighting, the Greek town appeared to be set on fire, 'the flames catching from house to house.'

'Without boast or vanity,' announced the preliminary puffs (the commercial advertising of the day) 'we may modestly say in the whole several scenes, movements and machines, it is in no way inferior even to any one opera yet seen in either of the Patent Houses.'

From 1711 to 1713, in the Little Piazza at Covent Garden, there existed the fashionable Punch's Theatre, run by Martin Powell, who presented a number of satires on contemporary society as well as burlesques on the new craze for Italian opera. Indeed *The Spectator* considered the opera at The King's Theatre in the Haymarket and that under the Little Piazza in Covent Garden to be 'at present the two leading diversions of the town.' Punch, descended from a long line of English clowns, was the star of the theatre, just as later he was to appear in the pantomimes, on horseback at Astley's, and eventually, in the nineteenth century, was to have a satirical journal named after him.

In a history of London theatre, as of theatre in general, it is all too easy to forget the important part played by the miniature theatre of puppet and marionette. The stage in Powell's booth was a replica of the major theatres of the day. It was lit by footlights—interestingly one of the earliest instances of their use—and mounted with side-wings, sky-pieces, and backcloths. The machines which operated the scenery and flying effects were copies of those invented by Inigo Jones for the court masques of the previous century.

Similar miniature theatres were to be found at the London fairs: Bartholomew Fair, May Fair, Tottenham Court Fair, the Welsh Fair, Mile End Fair, the Bow Green Goose Fair, the Hownslow Fair, all of which provided a variety of entertainment throughout the seventeenth and eighteenth centuries. The plays performed were mainly drolls, their story-lines drawn from ballad and chapbook, although Bartholomew Fair, especially in the seventeenth century, provided topical plays, often with political comment, satirical in tone, and performed both by marionettes and by live actors. In general, however, they were simple tales, full of dragons, witches and ghosts. New tales were also invented in melodramatic style more than half a century before the taste for melodrama developed at the theatres royal. The fairs also provided the equivalent of newsreels: spectacles depicting the events of the day. These, and similar experiments at Sadler's Wells, mark the first examples in England of documentary theatre.

The inn yards were the favourite sites for the play booths—whether for live actors or marionettes. One of the advantages of an inn yard was that coaches could drive up to the door and drop off those guests who did not want to be harried and hemmed in by the milling throngs—and pickpockets. The booths that were built at the fairs were not tents but barn-like structures made of wooden planking, as can be seen in Hogarth's famous painting of Southwark Fair. The size of the booths and their resemblance to the patented theatres was a matter of pride. In 1715, for example, the King's Players announced that they had erected the largest booth ever built at Bartholomew Fair, while Mrs Lee advertised that her booth was 'as near the perfection of a theatre as could be devised.'

Charles Dickens records that at Greenwich Fair, Richardson, whose booth seated a thousand, presented a melodrama (with three murders and a ghost), a pantomime, a comic song, an overture, and some incidental music, all done in five and twenty minutes. These melodramas and pantomimes gave many an actor his training. The stage career of James Barnes, a famous Pantaloon, began in Richardson's theatre at Bartholomew Fair, and he wrote, 'I am not ashamed to own it. Many others, who have prospered more than I, began there.' Increasingly, during the eighteenth century, established actors from the Patent Theatres came to act at the booth-theatres during the summer months when the main theatres were closed. Although the poorest of the booth-theatres were crowded and uncomfortable, the best were large, with steeply raked auditorium, and boxes. Eventually permanent buildings were erected to house them. The booth-theatres, with their elaborately staged shows, were well supported not merely by the lower but by the middle- and upper-classes, including the aristocracy and royalty. As the following verse (written 1738) indicates, the booth-theatres succeeded in being both best-sellers and editions de luxe:

> Each wooden house then groans to bear
> The populace that crowd the Fair . . . .
> The chambermaid and countess sit
> Alike admirers of the wit:
> The Earl and footman tête-à-tête
> Sit down contented in one seat.
> The music plays, the curtain draws,
> The Peer and Prentice clap applause.
> The house is filled with roaring laughter
> From lowest pit to highest rafter.

In 1738 a grand new Punch's Theatre opened above the old Tennis Court in James

Street off the Haymarket. Tennis courts had been adapted as playhouses since the middle of the seventeenth century, but this was the last to continue in use as a theatre. It was master-minded by Charlotte Charke, daughter of Colley Cibber. She enlisted the technical help of Yeates, a one-time partner of Martin Powell's son. Yeates was a regular exhibitor at the London fairs with large waxwork figures, and father and son were to become important proprietors of fairground theatrical booths.

Mrs Charke announced for the opening of Punch's Theatre a double bill of Shakespeare's *Henry VIII,* intermixed with a pastoral piece, *Damon and Phillida,* written by her father, which was being acted the very same night at Drury Lane. She promised that the christening of the young Princess Elizabeth in Shakespeare's play would be represented with dancing by Punch and his wife Joan. Ten plays were presented during this season, the most successful being Fielding's *The Covent Garden Tragedy*, a burlesque set in a Covent Garden brothel in which Punch appeared as the madame, 'being the first time in petticoats.' The plays selected for this season were all regularly acted in the human theatres.

There were other marionette theatres in London in the eighteenth century. Fielding, under the pseudonym of Madame de la Nash, presented a satirical puppet theatre in Panton Street in 1748, while Samuel Foote presented *The Primitive Puppet Show* at the Haymarket in 1773 as a burlesque of the sentimental comedies then prevalent. Between 1770 and 1780 puppet plays were also being presented at Hickford's Rooms in Panton Street, in Marylebone Gardens, and in Piccadilly. In January 1777 no fewer than four different puppet (i.e. marionette) theatres were playing at the same time in the West End. In November 1791, Joseph Haydn was present at one of these performances in the elegant little theatre called Variétés Amusantes, belonging to Lord Barrymore in Savile Row. He observed in his diary, 'the puppets were well managed, the singers bad, and the orchestra tolerably good.' The performances were billed as commencing at 8 p.m., doors open at 7 p.m. 'The theatre is well aired, and illuminated with wax' and, continued the playbill, 'refreshments to be had at the Rooms of the theatre. Boxes 5s., Pit 3s.'

By the 1720s the old practice of making a single play an evening's entertainment (whether at Rich's renovated Lincoln's Inn Fields or at Drury Lane) had been supplanted by Rich's theatrical evening, a mixture of full-length drama, with entr'acte entertainments of song and dance, followed by an afterpiece, often a farce, pantomime or short ballad opera.

A new form was given to pantomime in 1721 when, at Lincoln's Inn Fields, John Rich produced *The Magician or Harlequin A Director.* To dumb action were added transformation scenes and demonstrations of magic such as were regularly seen at Bartholomew Fair, given by the conjuror Fawkes. Palaces and temples were suddenly transformed into huts and cottages, trees converted to houses, colonnades to beds of tulips. The magician's tricks introduced by Rich were

1.   Wenzel Hollar's engraving showing the Bear Garden and The Globe (their names erroneously reversed by Hollar), *c.* 1644.

2.   William Hogarth's *The Idle 'Prentice Executed at Tyburn*. Hanging was a regular and popular theatrical spectacle, whether at Tyburn or at Execution Dock.

3.   The heart of London, in 1647, as now, straddles its main thoroughfare—the river Thames.

4.   Cock-fighting, *c.* 1739. This perennially popular sport has recently been illegally revived in England.

tectum

porticus

sedilia

orchestra

ingressus

mimorum
ædes

proscænium

planities sive arena

quintum sed dispari et structura, bestiarum conuectati
oni destinatum, in quo multi ursi, Tauri, et stupenda
magnitudinis canes, discretis cautis & septis aluntur, qui
ad

6.   Nell Gwyn, who started her career selling oranges in the theatre, progressed to acting, and finally became Charles II's mistress.

5.   A copy of de Witt's drawing of the interior of The Swan theatre, *c.* 1596, the only contemporary drawing of the interior of an Elizabethan playhouse.

7. Mrs Margaret Hughes, who became the first English actress on the professional stage when she played Desdemona in *The Moor of Venice* in December 1660.

8.   Ludgate, in the foreground, and, behind, St. Paul's Cathedral on fire in
September 1666 during the Great Fire of London.

9. *Southwark Fair* by William Hogarth. Miniature and booth-theatres were to be found at all the London fairs offering a variety of entertainment throughout the seventeenth and eighteenth centuries.

10. A typical scene at a London fair.

The MINOR.

Mr FOOTE as Mrs COLE.

My thoughts are fix'd upon a better place.
What, I suppose Mr Loader, you will be
for your old friend the black-ey'd Girl &c.

Act I.

Publish'd 26 July 1777, by T.Lowndes & Partners.

11.   Samuel Foote, one of the most inventive and colourful managers as well as a brilliant mimic, as Mrs Cole, 1777.

12. 'A Cruise to Covent Garden', 1806. Covent Garden and Drury Lane were surrounded by lanes and alleyways crowded with beggars and pickpockets: making a journey by sedan chair a hazardous venture.

13. The young Peg Woffington's famous visit to the great manager John Rich.

14.   The great actor David Garrick.

15.   The King and Queen of the Sandwich Islands attending Covent Garden theatre in 1824—the presence of royalty in the seventeenth and eighteenth centuries always helped to fill the house—a practice that was to continue.

16.   A side-box in 1781: an over-dressed and carefully manicured dandy
gossips with the ladies at the theatre.

17. The start of a riot at Covent Garden. Visitors from abroad repeatedly likened the behaviour of audiences at the theatre to that of a gathering at a bear garden.

18.　An early view of Sadler's Wells in 1720. One of the most colourful minor theatres, Sadler's Wells was opened as a water spa in 1683 by Dick Sadler.

19.　Sadler's Wells in 1792 after its alteration and enlargement in 1765.

A Lady, dancing an Allemand.   *The Merry Villagers.*   *A Lady Spinning.*   *The Marchioness of France going out in her carriage with Attendants.*

This Dog walks on any Leg at Command.   *Ladies of Quality going on a Visit.*   *The Death Warrant arrives and the little Deserter is prepared for Execution.*   *Storming the Castle.*

20. Scalioni's dancing dogs at Sadler's Wells—the entertainment that broke all box office records and made a profit of over £7,000 in 1784.

imitated by Drury Lane. In *Harlequin Dr Faustus*, Mephistopheles entered Faustus's study on a dragon breathing fire, while in a later scene devils appeared who tore Faustus to pieces, each flying off through the air with a piece of the dismembered magician in their hands.

Eventually the fashion for this form of entertainment became so prevalent that Garrick at Drury Lane in 1750, having to drop Shakespeare in favour of pantomime, commented bitterly in a prologue:

> Unwilling we must change the nobler scene,
> And in our turn present you Harlequin;
> Quit poets and set carpenters to work,
> Show gaudy scenes, or mount the vaulting Turk.
> For though we actors one and all agree
> Boldly to struggle for our vanity,
> If want comes on, importance must retreat:
> Our first great ruling passion is to—eat!

It was the pantomime that was to produce, in due course, at the beginning of the next century, the unique genius of Grimaldi or Joey the Clown.

In 1735 Henry Fielding, having taken over the management of the unpatented theatre, The Little Theatre in the Hay, announced 'The Great Mogul's Company of English Comedians who have dropped from the Clouds, Newly imported at the New Theatre in the Haymarket.' He presented *Pasquin,* A Drumstick Satire On The Times, Being the Rehearsal of Two Plays viz a Comedy Called The Election and A Tragedy Called The Life and Death of Common Sense.' It showed the supposed rehearsal of two plays, one dealing with country elections, with all their bribery and corruption, and the other dealing with the gross blundering of the law and the offences committed in its name against ordinary common sense. The two plays ran for fifty performances, a phenomenally long run in those days. With this success behind him, Fielding decided to tilt at the chief target of his reforming zeal, the First Minister, Sir Robert Walpole. His new play, *The Historical Register For The Year 1736*, presented at The Theatre in the Haymarket in 1737, was the cause of a revolution in the control of the theatres by the passing of the Licensing Act of 1737. This Act came about as a direct consequence of Fielding's play which was far more daring and outspoken on political matters than the previous *Pasquin*. Among many recognizable characters he created one called Quidam, a fiddler, who made people dance to his tune by means of bribes. There was not the slightest doubt that this was intended as a savage caricature of Walpole. At once Walpole drew up a bill which gave the Lord Chamberlain power to issue licences only for those theatres of which he approved, and to appoint an official for the reading and licensing of plays. The moment the Act became law, Walpole struck. Goodman's Fields Theatre was closed as well as The Little Theatre in the Hay, and Fielding was thrown out. The public, however, were on the side of Fielding and the Haymarket, and when in 1738 the Lord Chamberlain issued a licence to a company of French actors, permitting them to appear at the Haymarket, the crowds gathered in protest both outside and within the tiny theatre, patriotically singing 'The Roast Beef of Old England.' The authorities sent a detachment of guards under Colonel Pultenay in order to protect the French players, accompanied by Mr Justice Deveil, a magistrate, armed with a copy of the Riot Act. When he rose in his box and attempted to pronounce the occasion a riot, the matter was hotly disputed by members of the audience. Mr Justice Deveil insisted that it was the King's command that the performance should proceed. The curtain rose and immediately there was a roar from the audience for the French actors were seen to be standing, protected, between two rows of grenadier guards with fixed bayonets. The house insisted on the withdrawal of the soldiers. The magistrate agreed and, at a command, the Grenadiers wheeled and left the stage. One wit cried out, 'The British Army is on the retreat!' Once the troops had left, pit and gallery hurled dry peas onto the stage so that the French actors slithered and fell about. The Spanish and French ambassadors and their wives departed to loud boos and shouts from the remainder of the audience.

The London theatre was to see many such riots in its history, but in spite of the continued protest on this occasion the Licensing Act remained law.

Until the Patent Theatres' monopoly was abolished in 1843, many and ingenious were the efforts by managers of the 'minor' theatres, as they were called, to evade the law. One of the most inventive and colourful managers in the eighteenth century was Samuel Foote, a brilliant mimic, who took over The Little Theatre in the Hay at a time when it was almost derelict. On 27 April 1747 Londoners were startled to read the following announcement, 'At the Theatre in the Haymarket this day will be performed a Concert of Music, with which will be given gratis a new entertainment called *The Diversions of the Morning* and a farce taken from *The Old Bachelor*, entitled *"The Credulous Husband"—Fondlewife—Mr Foote*. And an Epilogue by the B–d–d Coffee House.' The latter was a deliberately provocative reference to the Bedford Coffee House where, as Foote knew, the show would be discussed and torn to pieces later in the day. It had the desired effect—the town turned up.

After a few musical items Foote appeared on stage, and under the pretence of conducting a rehearsal, he exposed the mannerisms and failings of the chief actors and actresses of the day—Quin, Ryan, Peg Woffington etc, but his final imitation, for which they were all waiting, was that of David Garrick. The success was immediate, and a tremendous epilogue was indeed spoken in the Bedford Coffee House that night as Foote had intended. He had, however, made a mistake by performing a play, *The Old Bachelor*. The next day, just as he was about to repeat the performance before a packed house, constables entered the theatre, summoned by the Patent Theatres, and dismissed the audience.

The following day Foote published a new announcement in the papers. 'On Saturday afternoon, exactly at 12 o'clock, at the New Theatre in the Haymarket, Mr Foote begs the favour of his friends to come and drink a dish of chocolate with him, and it is hoped there will be a great deal of company as diverting as possible. Tickets to be had for this entertainment at Georges Coffee House, Temple Bar, without which no one will be admitted. NB Sir Dilbury Diddle will be there and Lady Betty Frisk has absolutely promised . . .'

A large gathering of curious guests gathered at the Haymarket to meet their host and drink his chocolate. The curtain rose and Foote welcomed them. He explained that he was engaged in training some young actors. Under the pretence of putting them through their paces, he gave a long programme of his imitations. The event was a huge success and the law could not touch him. He was not performing a play, only conducting a rehearsal. All that he was selling was chocolate.

Foote's 'Diversions of the Morning' make him the true inventor of the matinée, as Macqueen Pope has observed. Foote eventually won a patent for his theatre, which he promptly named The Theatre Royal, although it was for the duration of his lifetime only.

Chapter four

The Eighteenth Century: II

Dick Sadler's musick house·Scalioni's performing dogs·Peg Woffington·Garrick·de Louterbourg

The eighteenth century was a period of increasing prosperity. As tradesmen became rich and accumulated money, so they wanted to improve their social standing. Since theatre-going was fashionable, they imitated the aristocracy. The changing audience inevitably helped to change fashions in playwriting, and the vicious comedies of the seventeenth century gave way to the more sentimental comedies of the eighteenth century. Increasingly it became a more middle-class theatre and the eighteenth-century workman was less able to afford to attend the theatre than his Elizabethan counterpart. Yet there is ample proof of his appetite for theatrical entertainment and it was this which helped to foster the 'underground' theatre of the eighteenth- and early nineteenth-century 'minor' theatres. So long as the Government legally limited the performance of legitimate drama to the more expensive patent houses, the 'minor' theatres continued to circumvent the latter by producing either pantomimes, concerts of music, or by setting a play to music so that it might come under the heading of what was defined as a burletta.

At such theatres as Goodman's Fields, the Haymarket, and at Sadler's Wells in Clerkenwell, the working man could occupy the same seat as at Drury Lane, but for sixpence instead of the usual shilling, for a full evening's entertainment which might, as at the Wells, include an aquatic show, an animal or variety show, a musical entertainment or a pantomime. That this kind of 'alternative' theatre was able to keep open in the face of the monopoly is due to the large following it had among the working-class. Such theatres were patently catering for a need as the Patent Theatres were not.

Attempts at Covent Garden and Drury Lane to abolish the custom of Half Price led to serious and prolonged rioting and the usual destruction of the furnishings. Riots nearly always began with the ushering of the ladies out of the pit. The harpsichords would then be smashed first, seats pulled up, box partitions splintered, mirrors cracked and hangings torn down. The managements were forced to yield to popular sentiment and, according to the time-honoured custom, those who were unable to come at the beginning of the evening's programme, or who could not afford the full price of admission, were admitted after the close of the third act of the principal item on the programme. It has to be remembered that the greater number of the labouring classes, and these included tailors, shopkeepers, etc, did not finish work until 8 p.m. In addition, the programme was so structured as to be in two parts, and it was the custom to place the lighter portion of the entertainment in the second half of the programme, after 7 p.m. Each half of the programme very often attracted a different audience. The farce in those days, which was placed in the second half of the programme, was not the sketchy thing it became by the 1880s but, as one German visitor in 1791 remarked, 'A unique feature . . . was the afterpiece, in which the greatest variety of entertainment was offered, and for which the seats, hitherto comparatively empty, were invariably filled to capacity; for after the first acts of the main play, the price of admission was reduced by half.' The working-class man, therefore, had he the leisure, could choose between half an evening at a Patent Theatre or a full evening, for the same money, at one of the 'minor' theatres.

One of the most colourful of such theatres was Sadler's Wells in Islington. In 1683, on the country footpath from Clerkenwell to Islington, Dick Sadler had opened a Musick House in which singers and entertainers amused the public. One day in the garden he discovered an ancient well, the water from which was found to possess mineral qualities. It was made into beer and proved so efficacious that London physicians began recommending it to their patients so that by the summer of 1685 some five hundred or more people frequented the Musick House every morning for the waters. Patients were recommended to drink the water early in the morning after a walk to Sadler's Wells. To make the walk more attractive Dick Sadler laid out ornamental gardens and arbours, and a marble basin for the water. He also built a long room with a stage at one end on the lawn outside the Musick House, and engaged tumblers, rope-dancers, and other entertainers to perform in the open air at no extra cost to the drinkers.

But Sadler's spring stopped flowing, so that his entertainments had to become the chief attraction and, after 1700, the waters were no longer advertised. Gradually standards deteriorated until by 1711 Sadler's Wells was referred to as 'a nursery of debauchery.' In 1745 it was included in a list of places condemned by the authorities who were determined to clean up such spots.

Things changed, however, in 1746, when the theatre was leased to Thomas Rosoman and Peter Hough, who reopened the Wells in April of that year and thereby started twenty years of prosperity for the old wooden theatre.

Rosoman realized the value of good variety and good music. He engaged the famous Rayner family of rope-dancers—Miss Rayner danced on the rope with a pair of candlesticks fixed to her feet. In 1750 Michael Maddox began a seven-year spell of popularity: he would stand on a wire, balanced on a coach wheel, and play the violin, the trumpet and the drum; or stand on his head on a swinging wire and fire off a brace of pistols at the same time.

They were long shows. To avoid the management being prosecuted for charging for theatrical entertainment, Rosoman's device for evading the law was to admit patrons on purchase of a pint of wine or punch. To help the sale of drinks he also sold shrimps.

By 1763 the entertainments had become so popular that Rosoman announced Sadler's Wells would be pulled down at the end of the season and rebuilt. In October of that year the old wooden theatre was destroyed and the new one was up and tiled within seven weeks at a cost of £4,225. The new enlarged brick theatre with its elegant iron gate and palisadoes, opened at 6 p.m. on Easter Monday, 8 April 1765, and though altered and enlarged at various times subsequently, it remained virtually the same to within a year or two of 1883. Its walls were still standing in 1927 and its last remains only taken down in 1938.

In 1771 Rosoman sold the remaining shares to a friend of Garrick, Thomas King, who made many alterations, raised the ceiling, increased the rake of the floor of the boxes and of the pit, improved ventilation and sight lines and, because he was an actor (his Lord Ogleby in *The Clandestine Marriage* was famous), introduced more dramatic entertainments as well as star billing. Gradually the Wells became fashionable. In Fanny Burney's novel, *Evelina*, published that year, when the London family are discussing where to take their country cousins, Mr Braughton asks the heroine:

> 'Pray, cousin, have you been to Sadler's Wells yet?'
>
> 'No, sir.'
>
> 'No? Why then you have seen nothing!'

By 1800 the Wells was able to announce that it was 'under the patronage of His Royal Highness, the Duke of Clarence', and so it remained for thirty years until the Duke became William IV. In its long history Sadler's Wells has seen a bizarre number of entertainments. The 1780s saw a hare beating a drum; two horses dancing a minuet; a singing duck; and the Learned Pig which, by means of typographical cards, set out names, calculated the number of people present, told the time, and answered sundry other questions. Of this pig Samuel Johnson wrote, 'Had he been illiterate he had long since been smoked into hams . . . . Now he is visited by the philosopher and the politician . . . gazed at with the eye of wonder . . . and gratified with the murmur of applause.' But the entertainment that broke all box office records and made for the management a profit of over £7,000 occurred in 1784. This was Scalioni's troupe of performing dogs acting *The Deserter* under their leader, Moustache. In his *Life and Times,* Frederick Reynolds wrote, 'Moustache as the Deserter! I see him now, in his little uniform, military boots, with smart musket and helmet, cheering and inspiring his fellow soldiers to follow him up scaling ladders and storm the fort. The roars, the barking and confusion, which resulted from this attack, may be better imagined than described.'

In 1740 there arrived from Dublin a young actress named Peg Woffington:

> That excellent Peg
> Who showed such a leg
> When lately she dressed in men's clothes—
> A creature uncommon,
> Who's both man and woman
> And the chief of the belles and the beaux!

The manager whom she set out to see soon after her arrival was John Rich who, after managing the Lincoln's Inn Fields for twenty years, had built Covent Garden Theatre in 1732, licensed to present legitimate drama. There were six Royal Command performances within the first season and it rapidly became a powerful theatre. Peg Woffington called at his home nineteen times before finally she was admitted.

'The great manager, as Woffington first saw him, was lolling in ungraceful ease on a sofa, holding a play in one hand, and in the other a tea cup from which he sipped frequently,' observed a writer in *The Dublin Review*. 'Around him were seven and twenty cats of all sizes, colours and kinds, Toms and Tabithas, old cats and kittens, tortoise shells, Maltese, brindles, white, black, and yellow cats of every description. Some were frisking over the floor, others asleep on the rug; one was licking the buttered toast on his breakfast plate, another was engaged in drinking the cream for his tea, two cats lay on his knee, one was asleep on his shoulder, and another sat demurely on his head. Peg Woffington was astounded at the sight. Rich, to her mind, had for years been the greatest man in the world. The menagerie of grimalkins, amid which he lay so carelessly, was so different an environment from her conception of the study of the Covent Garden manager that she was embarrassed into silence.'

The London to which Peg had come was the London of Hogarth. Covent Garden and Drury Lane were surrounded by lanes and alley ways, crowded with beggars and pickpockets, through which the sedan-chairs had to thrust their way. It was a period of extreme dandyism when men often wore extravagantly high wigs—Colley Cibber once brought down the house by coming on stage followed by a wig so large that it had to be carried in a sedan chair. The women did not hesitate to compete and, as the height of their periwigs rose, the roofs of the sedan-chairs had to be raised in order to accommodate these enormous structures of wool and horsehair which, often and unknown to the wearers, also accommodated nests of mice.

The dandies flaunted nosegays of artificial flowers, wore high-heeled shoes, thrust their hands into muffs, and sniffed at perfume bottles as they sat gossiping with the ladies in their boxes at the theatre.

Such an audience was gathered on the evening of 6 November 1740 at the hour of six o'clock, at Covent Garden, for the London debut of Peg Woffington. In the royal box, under a canopy of scarlet silk, adorned with gold tassels, sat the Prince and Princess of Wales. 'In the pit, as usual, sat the students of the Inns of Court, the men about town, the young fellows from the Universities, with their periwigs, swords, ruffles, and snuff boxes: glib compliments on their lips . . . and much knowledge of stage affairs in their heads, by which they would presently, over a glass of wine, try their Irish actress and pronounce judgement upon her. Presently when the fiddles had played their last notes, and the candles had been judiciously snuffed, up went the heavy green curtain; then a silence fell upon the house, broken only by the fluttering of fans and the snapping of snuff boxes.'

The house that night, continues Fitzgerald Molloy, the observer, was charmed by Peg's first entrance as the feminine Sylvia but it was when she came on in disguise, dressed as 'a pretty gentleman about town' that the house went wild. Thereafter, backstage, before, during and after every performance Peg's dressing room was besieged by the beaux.

In spite of Queen Anne's attempt to rid the stage of the beaux, players still had to fight their way through crowds even to get on stage. In Johnson's day 'twelve penny stools' on the stage itself were still being sold. On one occasion Peg Woffington played Cordelia clasped around the waist by an amorous gallant, while Mrs Cibber, in *Romeo and Juliet,* frequently thrilled the audience to enthusiasm—including the hundred or so who were with her in the tomb. Tate Wilkinson in his *Memoirs* recalls how 'Mr Quin, aged sixty-five, with the heavy dress of Falstaff (notwithstanding the impatience of the audience to see their old acquaintance) was several minutes before he could pass through their numbers that wedged and hemmed him in, he was so cruelly encompassed around.'

When Peg Woffington went to work at Drury Lane in 1741 she found it worse there. There was only one entrance to the pit and boxes on each side of the stage, and many of the beaux who crowded these doors delighted in impeding the passage of the players. They would also bandy words with the gallery, 'who showed their resentment by dispersing golden showers of oranges and half-eaten pippins to the infinite terror of the ladies seated in the pit, where they were so closely wedged as to preclude the possibility of securing a retreat.' Others sat on the front of the stage in rows, three or four deep. A performer could hardly move sometimes without striking a member of the audience.

In vain were the beaux warned off the stage, many of whom would force their way into the theatres without paying. In 1721, during a performance of *Macbeth* at Lincoln's Inn Fields, a titled occupant of one of the boxes crossed the stage, during a scene between Lady Macbeth and her husband, and exchanged greetings with another gallant lolling in the wings. Rich, who was then the manager, stepped forward to remonstrate, whereupon he was struck in the face. Rich returned the blow. Swords were drawn as other beaux rallied round but Rich, backed by his actors—Quin, Ryan, and Walker—also with swords, drove their opponents out of the theatre. They returned, however, with reinforcements and after doing much damage attempted to set fire to the theatre. The military were called in, the offenders sent for trial, and the theatre closed for nearly a week. To prevent such outrages in future, an armed guard was ordered by the King to attend all future performances at either of the Patent Houses. (A guard was mounted regularly at Drury Lane until as late as 1896.) Audiences were generally more volatile and this was as much part of going to the theatre as watching the play. Those in the pit were given to expressing loudly their criticisms, much to the entertainment of those in the gallery. Mrs Parsons expressed the fervent hope that it was during the interval, and not during the play, that 'Boswell, one night, entertained the Drury Lane audience prodigiously by lowing in the pit like a cow. "Encore the cow!" cried the galleries till, finally, the Rev. Dr Hugh Blair found it necessary to restrain his young friend's very inferior imitations of other animals by the caustic recommendation "My dear sir, I would *confine* myself to the cow!"'

Boswell, in his London Journal, for 8 December 1762, records, 'At night I went to Covent Garden and saw *Love In A Village* by Isaac Bickerstaffe, a new comic opera for the first night. I liked it much. I saw it from the gallery but I was first in the pit. Just before the overture began to be played, two Highland officers came in. The mob in the gallery roared out, "No Scots! No Scots! Out with them!", hissed and pelted them with apples. My heart warmed to my countrymen, my Scottish blood boiled with indignation. I jumped up on the benches, roared out, "Damn you, you rascals!", hissed, and was in the greatest rage. I went close to the officers and asked them what regiment they were of. They told me Lord John Murray's and they were just come from Havana. "And this," said they, "is the thanks that we get—to be hissed when we come home. If it was French what could they do worse? The rudeness of the English vulgar is terrible. This indeed is the liberty they have: the liberty of bullying."'

Even as late as 1791 a German visitor observed, 'The uproar before the play begins is indescribable . . . not only orange peels but sometimes glasses of water or other liquids are thrown from the gallery into pit and boxes, so that frequently spectators are wounded and their clothing soiled. In short, such outrages are committed in the name of freedom that one forgets one is in a playhouse which claims in its advertisements the title of a Royal Theatre. In Germany such disorder would never be tolerated even at a marionette theatre in a village inn. At Drury Lane I wished to look around at the gallery in order to examine its structure, but a heap of orange peels, striking me with considerable force in the face, robbed me of all curiosity. The best plan is to keep your face turned to the stage, and thus quietly submit to the hail of oranges on your back.'

Samuel Rodgers, an American visitor, remembering the one time he had seen Garrick act, tells of the long waiting in a dark crowded passage on his way to the pit and then, when the doors were opened, 'a dangerous trial of skill ensues; every person endeavours to enter first; the space is clogged; and pushing, screams and execrations follow.'

An entry in Richard Cross's *Diary* for 26 December 1757 shows that the upper gallery passages were even more dangerous. 'This night by the crowd upon the upper Gallery stairs two women and a man were killed,' while another contemporary described 'constant disputes often terminating in blows . . . heated bodies stripped of outward garments, furious faces, with others grinning terribly.'

The presence of royalty always helped to fill a house but other attractions were continually being sought. Thus, on 16 October 1736, the notorious bone-setter, Mrs Mapp—who daily travelled from Epsom in a coach to set bones or to lecture at the Grecian Coffee House—was billed as honouring with her presence a performance of a play entitled *Husband's Relief*.

On another occasion it was announced that 'Four Kings' would attend a performance of *Macbeth*; these were American Indian chiefs to whom the courtesy title of 'Kings' had been applied. The theatre was correspondingly packed that night 'to see the Kings' who were placed in the centre box. Here they were invisible to the occupants of the gallery, who loudly demanded their money back unless they could see the distinguished visitors. After some haggling with the audience, the manager finally placed four chairs on the stage and the Indian 'Kings' gravely descended from their box to a chorus of loud cheers.

What is especially interesting during the eighteenth century is the often intimate relationship between actors, royalty and audience. Once, the young King of Denmark, a frequent visitor to the London theatre in the 1760s, and who subsequently married the sister of George III, fell asleep during a command performance of *Jane Shore,* much to the amusement of the audience but not of Mrs Bellamy who was playing Alicia. When she came to the words, 'Oh, thou false Lord!', she approached the royal box and spoke them so loudly that the King awoke, startled, protesting that he would never marry a woman with such a loud voice!

On another occasion he went to see Garrick play the part of Ranger in *The Suspicious Husband*. The pit was so crowded and hot that all the men took off their coats and sat in their shirt-sleeves, even though they were in the royal presence. It was so hot that many men fainted. When Garrick appeared, the audience roared with applause and the King rose, assuming it was for him, and Garrick had to wait until he sat down.

It was on the evening of 19 October 1741, in a half-empty theatre in the East End, at Goodman's Fields Theatre, that the free offering between the musical interludes was a performance of Shakespeare's *Richard III*. The actor was David Garrick, aged twenty-four, untrained in acting, newly arrived in London from Lichfield. Within weeks he was the talk of the town and hundreds were turned away nightly from the little theatre. Alexander Pope, who had given up playgoing, was one of the many celebrities who made the trip down to the East End. He came three times. 'That young man,' he said, 'never had his equal and will never have a rival.'

Since the death of Thomas Betterton actors had fallen into a mechanical sing-song cadence. Garrick always avoided any suggestion of rant or sing-song. He himself is said to have remarked that Quin was able to find many words on which to lay emphasis where he, Garrick, could fine none.

From a salary of £1 a night Garrick's remuneration went up to a half of the profits. The Patent Theatres remained empty when he played at Goodman's Fields and accordingly the patentees made terms with Giffard, the manager, under threat of closing his theatre, and Garrick was brought to Drury Lane, where his salary was fixed at £600 per annum, being a hundred more than that of Quin who, until then, had been the highest paid player.

A few years later, on 14 November 1746, Garrick was to act with Quin in *The Fair Penitent*. This was the greatest theatrical event that had occurred for years and 'when the actor of the old school and he of the new met on the stage, in the second act, the audience who now first saw them, as they had long wished, to see them, face to face, absolutely disconcerted them by a hurricane of greeting . . . . When it had passed, every word was listened to breathlessly, every action marked. Some were won by the grand emphasis and moral dignity of Quin; others by the grace and happy wickedness of Garrick. Between them it was difficult to award the palm of supreme distinction to either.'

Garrick came off so well in this encounter with Quin that he had no fears of trying a contest with a much praised actor of his own generation, Spranger Barry.

The Drury Lane season of 1747–8 found Garrick joint patentee with Lacy. In this season London audiences saw Macklin's Shylock; Barry's Hamlet, Othello, and Pierre; while Garrick drew full houses with his performances as Abel Drugger, Lear, Richard, Hamlet and Macbeth. But the greatest attraction of all was when Garrick and Barry played together in *Venice Preserv'd*.

In 1750, Garrick and Barry played rival Romeos, Garrick at Drury Lane and Barry at Covent Garden. It was a duel which lasted for twelve performances, Garrick topping the contest with a thirteenth, until the audiences were thoroughly tired of it, as was evidenced by a verse which went the round of the town:

> Well, what's tonight? says angry Ned
> As up from bed he rouses.
> 'Romeo again!' and shakes his head,
> 'A plague on both your houses!'

On one occasion, at Mrs Bellamy's request, 'Romeo, Romeo, wherefore art thou Romeo?', a witty Irish voice called out 'Faith, because Barry's at the other house!'

Garrick's influence on London's theatre was not confined, however, to the impact made by his acting. In 1747 he became joint patentee of Drury Lane.

Changes in the running of the theatre were soon introduced, such as punctuality at rehearsals, the accurate learning of lines, etc. His reforms also included the spectators. He finally succeeded, as others had not, in achieving 'the decency of a cleared stage.' Garrick also announced that admissions would no longer take place behind the scenes. At the peak of that first season, Lord Hubbard's party damned Garrick's production of *The Foundling* ostensibly because 'it ran too long and they wanted variety of entertainments,' but, according to the prompter, 'the main cause of their anger, in spite of their excuses, was their being refused admittance behind the scenes.'

It was in fact another fifteen years before Garrick accomplished a complete reformation and in order to replace the lost seats, he reduced the depth of the apron stage, taking it closer to the proscenium arch.

Garrick's other major area of reform was in stage design. In 1771, on a visit to Paris, he met Phillipe Jacques de Loutherbourg, a painter of battle-scenes and romantic landscapes. Garrick offered him the post of scenic designer at Covent Garden.

What he did for Garrick was to create a real picture stage. He abolished the chandeliers above the apron stage and placed a series of lights behind the proscenium which meant that the scenery was better lit. This, in turn, forced the actors back onto the stage, behind the proscenium arch. He developed the use of wings and borders, and introduced cut cloths—backdrops with irregular pieces cut from them to reveal further vistas beyond, which improved the effect of perspective and added to the illusion of outdoor scenes. He was also fond of transparent scenery: the moon, for example, would be cut out of the canvas backcloth and replaced by gauze, lit from behind. In addition he invented a 'new device whereby the fleeting effect of various colours on a landscape was produced by means of silk screens working on pivots before concentrated light in the wings.' Many of his ideas were to find fruition in the nineteenth-century predilection for dioramas. The general public flocked to see his innovations and, when Garrick retired in 1776, Richard Sheridan, who succeeded as manager of Drury Lane, continued to employ de Loutherbourg. In his play, *The Critic*, Sheridan refers to him by name, remarking 'as to the scenery, the miraculous powers of Mr de Loutherbourg's pencil are universally acknowledged.'

The importance which landscape painting began to assume in the theatre is shown by the fact that the Drury Lane pantomime of 1779 was specially written round the scenery which de Loutherbourg had devised while on holiday in Derbyshire. It is significant that most of his work was done for pantomimes and had little to do with the legitimate drama. This was to come in the next century with the Cecil B. de Mille-type productions of Charles Kean.

De Loutherbourg grew so dissatisfied with the insistent demands of actors to be considered more important than the scenery (and the eighteenth century was one of great actors) that he withdrew to create one of the most unusual theatres in London's history, the celebrated *Eidophusikon,* a theatre that would have delighted Gordon Craig, and the Bauhaus; one from which the actor and the playwright were entirely banished, the 'play' consisting solely of scenic effects. Although the stage on which he worked was little more than six feet wide and eight feet in depth, yet such was his skill that he created the illusion of infinite depth, complete with intricate sound and lighting effects. Gainsborough was so enchanted with the *Eidophusikon* that he used to spend evening after evening there. De Loutherbourg also introduced a new art, that of picturesque sound for the theatre, an art that was subsequently to be further developed by the Moscow Art Theatre with its orchestras of sound effects men. The popularity of De Loutherbourg's theatre, however, lasted only two years, and thereafter he devoted himself to landscape painting.

As Garrick began the 1775–6 season he was tired and unwell. As Macready and others were also to learn, the stresses and strains of management of a large theatre such as Drury Lane or Covent Garden, combined with staging a great variety of productions, and playing in swift succession a series of leading roles, took their toll, and Garrick announced his retirement. *Exit Roscius!* Drury Lane audiences heard the news for the first time in a prologue spoken by Thomas King. This was followed by a series of farewell performances in each of his famous roles. Places for these performances became harder and harder to get. 'The eagerness of people to see him,' wrote Hannah More in a letter, 'is beyond anything you can have idea of. You will see half a dozen duchesses and countesses of a night, in the upper boxes: for the fear of not seeing him at all, has humbled those who used to go, not for the purpose of seeing, but of being seen; and they now curtsey to the ground for the worst places in the house.'

The management of Drury Lane passed to Thomas King and the mantle of Garrick to John Philip Kemble who, in 1788, also took over the management of the theatre on King's retirement. Kemble set out with high hopes to reform what had been called 'the slaughter-house of dramatic poetry,' but the contrariness of its proprietor, Richard Brinsley Sheridan, drove him and his sister, Sarah Siddons, from the theatre.

In 1792 Drury Lane was rebuilt to accommodate 3,611 spectators and opened in April 1794. Without the aid of gas or electricity by way of illumination, it must have been difficult for any but those close to the stage to see the actors. As the actors retreated further onto and upstage, so they dwindled in size and, ultimately, in importance. Inevitably, melodrama and spectacle began to replace the legitimate drama. It was, in any case, a period when audiences seemed in search of the spectacular. In 1772 Astley started his circus near Westminster Bridge, which in turn was followed by his Amphitheatre, which was to be famous throughout the world for almost a century. There was also Charles Dibdin's Royal

Circus and Equestrian Philharmonic Academy. This was remarkable in that it possessed both a circle (as the ring was called) and a stage. The pit boxes and gallery formed an oval with the circle in the centre and the stage at one end. Above the stage the roof opened so that, when required, fireworks could be let off. Here, ballets, horse shows, and burlesque pantomimes were staged. It is during this period that we find a craze for documentary theatre, staged with all the verisimilitude of a waxwork display, and the grandeur of opera. Among a number of such productions, *The Fall of Bastille* was staged both at Sadler's Wells and at The Royal Circus. The Bastille fell on 14 July 1789, and on 31 August Sadler's Wells presented *Gallic Freedom or Vive La Liberté,* showing 'The first assembling of the Bourgeoisie in the Faubourg St Martin . . . the Manner of their proceeding to the Assault of the BASTILLE and their previous Conference with the Governor . . . the Massacre of the Citizens who passed the Drawbridge . . . the Cannonade and the General Attack . . . the actual Descent of the Soldiers and Citizens by Torch Light into the SUBTERRANEAN DUNGEONS . . . the Discovery of the unfortunate Objects confined in the horrid recesses of the Place . . . .' This new custom of reproducing a recent event on the stage was to continue at the Wells in one form or another for some twenty-five years and the accuracy of the representations was always scrupulous.

On 23 August 1793, Marie Antoinette was removed to her new prison in the Conciergerie and the stage presentation of the 'persecution of an unfortunate female who was once the envy and admiration of Europe,' *Les Innocens Infermées or The Royal Prisoners,* was introduced at the Wells by Mrs Parker, a dancer, who 'performed admirably and drew tears from the whole audience. Her prison scene . . . where she throws herself on a bed of straw, with the effect of dropping the curtain to Storace's *Tune of Lullaby,* had a wonderful effect.'

These particular productions, stemming from those in the puppet- and booth-theatres of the fairs, reveal the theatre in its educational role. The next century, with its abundance of Scientific Exhibitions, Readings, Dioramas and Panoramas, and Waxworks, was to coincide with the emergence of a new electorate as well as, from the 1850s onwards, with the spread of education, the mass circulation of newspapers, the advent of the lending libraries, and the arrival of the steam train.

The end of the eighteenth century, however, held little hint of the fundamental changes that were to occur in the next hundred years, witnessing rather a mass passion for amusement. There were prize-fights, cock-fights, bull- and bear-baiting, horse racing, gambling. A group of gallants would get up a party to see a woman hanged. Crowds would visit Bedlam and pay to laugh at the antics of the insane, while at the opera the entrance of Beau Brummell would be a signal for everyone of quality in the house to focus their opera-glasses upon his box. Conscious of this, like royalty, he would grace the occasion and acknowledge the attention.

During the reign of George III the wealth and power of the nation lay in the hands of a small, snobbish group of about one hundred families, whilst a vast majority, having deserted the rural areas and gravitated towards the city, lived in conditions of appalling poverty, among thieves, pickpockets and murderers. London had become the biggest (its population swollen to 750,000) and richest city of the western world. Against this background of wealth and fashion, symbolized by Beau Brummell and the Prince Regent, and shadowed by the degradation of the working-classes, the figure of the mad King stands dramatically at the centre of the stage Roaming about the palace in a purple bathrobe, deaf and practically blind, talking ceaselessly to himself, his reason gone and muttering unintelligible sounds, he was to provide in the twentieth century the inspiration for a 'theatre piece' by the composer Peter Maxwell Davies, entitled *Songs of a Mad King*.

'All history,' says Thackeray, 'presents no sadder figure than that of the old man addressing imaginary parliaments, reviewing fancied troops, holding ghostly courts.' Banned as it was from the stage during the King's reign, life had produced a King Lear more real than any yet seen upon the stage of London's theatre.

Chapter five

The Nineteenth Century : I

*young Roscius·the Old Prices war dance·burlettas·theatre in the
suburbs*

'The town is mad: young Roscius, like all prodigies, is the talk of everyone. I have
not seen him, and perhaps never may. I have no curiosity to see him, as I well
know what is within the compass of a boy of fourteen; and as to real acting, it is
like historical painting: no boy's work.' Thus William Blake, then living in
London, writing to William Hayley on 25 April 1805 about Master Betty.

During the autumn of 1804, the curiosity of London's theatregoers was first
aroused by rumours of the amazing *enfant prodigue* who was taking the provinces,
as well as Ireland and Scotland, by storm. In Edinburgh he had played for fourteen
nights to packed houses, breaking all previous records, while in Stockport the
people rang the church bells to celebrate the news of his agreement to give an
extra performance. The public demand for him was prodigious—as were the
profits. It is little wonder that the announcement of Master Betty's first
appearance in London was anticipated as a major theatrical event. On 1 December
1804, the day of his debut at Covent Garden as Selim in *Barbarossa,* at ten o'clock
in the morning, the crowds began to mass outside the theatre. (It was not until
1870 that queuing became an English habit, acquired from the Continent—the
word queue meaning 'tail'.) By early afternoon the crowd numbered thousands
and stretched out 'in long, thick-wedged, impenetrable columns.' So alarmed was
the management that guards were sent for, to control the crowds when the doors
opened. But nothing could stop the pandemonium. 'The rush was terrific,'
described *The Daily Advertiser* the following day. 'In the space of a few minutes
the two galleries . . . seemed as one solid mass. Gentlemen who knew there were no
places untaken in the boxes, paid for admission and poured from the front boxes
into the pit in twenties and thirties at a time. Even after the pit was crammed, the
gentlemen crowded the front boxes . . . in spite of the ventilators, the heat was so
terrific that men and women fainted.'

The audience had an hour and a half to wait before the performance was due to
begin, and even longer before they had their first sight of the young Roscius, who
did not appear until mid-way through the second act; until then, there was such a
hubbub that the play might as well have been a pantomime. When at last Master
Betty stepped before the audience, there was an explosion of applause, of a kind

that would be heard later in the century for such great actors as Edmund Kean, William Charles Macready and Henry Irving; but, as Giles Playfair observes, the audience that night at Covent Garden had not come to judge their idol but to affirm their faith in his supremacy.

For the remainder of that season, and most of the next, all London was at his feet. He broke all previous box office records. The hysteria surrounding him was akin to that for a pop star in the twentieth century, yet it is clear that, judged as a relatively inexperienced boy actor, with a still unbroken voice, he must have had an extraordinary talent. The mere technical feat of being able to make himself heard in a theatre which was nearly twice the size of the present Drury Lane, without the aid of any amplification, is remarkable in itself. He had a prodigious memory, carrying some ten major parts in his repertoire, including those of Romeo, Hamlet, Richard III, and Tancred in James Thomson's Sicilian tragedy, *Tancred and Sigismunda*. He had been excellently coached (his scripts are packed with minute stage directions as to moves, gestures and speech patterns); above all, he loved acting, and his natural beauty and grace were entirely unselfconscious. Hazlitt, who saw him play the Young Norval in *Douglas,* the part for which he was most remembered, wrote, long afterwards, 'Master Betty's acting was a singular phenomenon, but it was also as beautiful as it was singular . . . he seemed almost like some "gay creature of the elements," moving about gracefully, with all the flexibility of youth and murmuring Aeolian sounds with plaintive tenderness. I shall never forget the way in which he repeated the line in which Young Norval says, speaking of the fate of his two brothers, "And in my mind happy was he that dies." The tones fell and seemed to linger on the air.'

On 4 March 1805, he played Romeo for the first time at Drury Lane. On 14 March he played Hamlet. 'This is finer than Garrick,' whispered Fox to Samuel Rogers during the play scene that night. The audience included, typically, Canning, Fox, the Duke of Devonshire, and the First Minister, William Pitt. It is interesting that his following was largely male. 'His dressing room,' observed James Northcote, 'was crowded as full as it could contain of all the court of England and happy were those who could get in at the time his father was rubbing his naked body from the perspiration after the exertion in performing his part on the stage.' Mrs Charles Mathews found it 'offensively amusing . . . to listen to the enthusiastic ecstasies of the noble visitors who came nightly to the green room to gaze upon the boy wonder and haply to kiss the garment hem of the Betty, who, had his person been as feminine as his name, could not have had more fervent male adorers, some of whom were almost impious in their enthusiasm.'

The androgynous quality of Master Betty, a more familiar phenomenon in the twentieth-century pop scene, enables us, however, to understand something of the sexual intensity and emotional appeal of the Elizabethan boy actors who played the female roles:

> Sirrah, go you to Bartholomew, my page,
> And see him dress'd in all suits like a lady . . .
> I know the boy will well usurp the grace
> Voice, gait and action of a gentlewoman!

Such a boy, uniting innocence and voluptuousness, clothed in male attire even, and Shakespeare's heroines are more often in male than female attire—appearing much as Master Betty does in the portraits of him as the Young Norval, can easily be imagined as Viola, disguised as Cesario, saying:

> 'I am all the daughters of my father's house,
> And all the brothers too . . .

The success of Master Betty led to a rush of imitations, from Miss Feron, aged eight, known as the Infant Billington (after Mrs Billington an opera singer); Miss Lee Sugg, aged seven, known as the young Roscia; Master Brown, aged thirteen, known as the Ormskirk Roscius; Master Mori, aged eight, known as the Young Orpheus; Master Byrne, aged nine, known as the Infant Vestris; Master Saunders, aged fourteen, known as the Infant Clown. There were others also, from the Infant Hercules, the Infant Candle-Snuffer, the Comic Roscius, to Miss Mudie, an eight-year-old child whose appearance in adult roles, as mistress and wife, set an all-time record for absurdity in the annals of theatre history.

On 12 September 1808, the year in which Master Betty, having retired from the stage, entered Christ's College, Cambridge, as a commoner, a new season opened at Covent Garden, with a return of the great actress, Mrs Sarah Siddons, and her brother, John Philip Kemble, also the manager of the theatre, in *Macbeth*. Eight days later, at four in the morning, the theatre was destroyed by fire. Most of the theatre's scenery, wardrobe, manuscripts and records, were burned. The loss was estimated at over £150,000 and only a small part of this was met by the insurance companies. For John Philip Kemble, at the age of fifty-one, it seemed a disaster: after only five seasons his theatre was destroyed, and he had to start all over again from scratch.

James Boaden, the writer, made an early call on Kemble, whom he found sitting in tears upon a sofa. On seeing him, Kemble exclaimed, 'Oh, Mr Boaden, we are totally ruined, and have the world to begin again.'

Five months later, on the night of 24 February 1809, Drury Lane, which had been totally rebuilt, and installed with tanks of water in the roof in the event of fire, was also burned to the ground. Like a Job's comforter, James Boaden (who rarely missed a theatrical occasion) was early on the scene. 'I hastened from my present house as soon as the news reached me, and stood in the centre of Russell Street, in a state of perspiration from the intense heat, while the water from the plugs was flowing over my feet. I saw the Apollo (a figure that stood on the roof of the theatre) sink in flames into the building; and then returned home, cheerless, and gloomy, to reflect upon the scene I had beheld.'

A message was sent to the House of Commons, which was sitting late, to break the news to Sheridan (who was then the manager of Drury Lane), who was waiting to make an important speech on the Spanish War. Two members proposed that the House should be adjourned 'in delicate attention to the loss sustained by so distinguished a member,' but Sheridan insisted upon their business being first concluded.

It was a shattering blow for Sheridan for whom the theatre represented well over a quarter of a million pounds worth of his and his partners' capital, especially as it had been insured for only about a quarter of that sum. When the House rose, Sheridan went to the Piazza Coffee House, accompanied by the Duke of York, where he sat calmly drinking wine and watching the blaze, which could be seen for miles around. When his friends urged him to return home, he protested, jesting, 'What? May not a man warm his hands at his own fireside?'

Immediately following the destruction of Covent Garden, a public subscription, headed by King George III and the Duke of York, had been launched, with the Duke of Cumberland (one of Kemble's admirers) contributing £19,000; while in 1810, a company, headed by Samuel Whitbread, was formed by order of Parliament, to rebuild Drury Lane by subscription. The architect was Wyatt and the new theatre was opened on 10 October 1812.

The new Covent Garden theatre was opened on 18 September 1809. The cost of this vast theatre was so high that the management decided to raise the prices, from six shillings to seven shillings for the boxes, and from three shillings and sixpence for the pit to four shillings; while the third tier, usually reserved for the public, was converted into private boxes at a rental of £300 a year. The gallery price was left unchanged, but the new gallery was so far up and the slope so steep that only the legs of the performers could be seen by the spectators in the gallery.

On the night of the opening, audience and actors stood to sing loyally the National Anthem, but, the moment it was ended, pandemonium broke loose. As John Philip Kemble stepped forward proudly on to the stage of his new theatre, he was greeted with a tempest of hissing, shouting and whistling, which continued throughout the performance of *Macbeth* that followed. Reiterated shouts of 'Old Prices! Old Prices!' greeted both Kemble and Mrs Siddons each time they appeared on stage. The noise was such that five hundred soldiers were dispatched to the gallery, but the rioters climbed down to the lower galleries, the sight of the soldiers merely increasing the antagonism of the house. 'It was a noble sight,' said *The Times,* 'to see so much just indignation in the public mind.' Most of the women in the private boxes left early in the evening. The shouting rioters stood with their backs to the stage, while the actors continued doggedly with their performance of *Macbeth* and, after it, a musical farce, *The Quaker.* When the programme was over, and the audience still refused to leave, Kemble sent for the police (Bow Street being opposite the theatre as it is today). This aroused the rioters to even greater protest so that the constables tactfully withdrew. It was not until two in the morning that the audience finally dispersed.

Night after night, week after week, the Old Price Riots continued, except that, after the first night, the rioters only came in at Half Price time. The inside of the theatre resembled a fairground with its banners and placards painted with slogans. Protests were made nightly against the exorbitant salaries received by the Kembles and 'their clothes on their backs worth £500' said *The Times*. Magistrates appeared on stage to read the Riot Act while lawyers addressed the house from the boxes, encouraging the rioters. Pigs were brought into the theatre to add their snorts of protest to the general cacophony of post-horns, rattles, trumpets, bugles, bells and whistles, while one man regularly took his seat every night with a large dustman's bell, which he rang determinedly. A coffin was carried in, inscribed 'Here lies the body of New Prices, who died of the whooping cough September 23rd 1809, aged six days.' They continued to whoop it up for another sixty-four days.

At the end of each performance the audience would unite in singing a parody of God Save the King:

> God save Great Johnny Bull,
> Long live our Noble Bull,
> God save John Bull—
> Send him victorious,
> Loud and uproarious,
> With lungs like Boreas,
> God save John Bull!

Pigeons were released from baskets to indicate that the public were not to be 'pigeoned'. Badges with the symbol O.P. were manufactured. People raced up and down the pit benches while the play was in progress, and roared with laughter when Charles Kemble, in *Richard III*, fell flat on his face. Men appeared wearing false noses, others appeared in drag, until the atmosphere was like a carnival. The O.P. War Dance was inaugurated and became a nightly ritual, which many came to see instead of the play.

After the performance the rioters would proceed nightly through the streets to make further protests before the offices of those newspapers which did not support their case but were on the side of the management. Always their last port of call would be 89 Great Russell Street, the home of John Philip Kemble, for whom their greatest venom was reserved. On the fiftieth night a celebration was held, and women who came wearing O.P. medals were loudly cheered. Men who had lost their hats in the previous night's fray turned up in nightcaps.

Unlike earlier riots, however, no damage was done to the theatre, and the whole affair was, in fact, conducted in a spirit of fun, the combatants declaring that they would obtain their end by perseverance. After three months of rioting, Kemble was finally obliged to accept the O.P. terms and to make a public apology from the stage which was greeted by loud applause and the hoisting of a placard in the pit bearing the words 'We are satisfied!' Thus ended the famous O.P. war. When, at the beginning of the next season, Kemble tried to break his promise by maintaining half the number of private boxes, the riots began all over again and he swiftly withdrew. Ultimately, however, the house proved unpopular because it was too large. The public could not easily hear and the stage was more suited to spectacle and melodramas. As Richard Cumberland had written in 1806, 'Since the stages of Covent Garden and Drury Lane have been so enlarged in their dimensions to be henceforward theatres for spectators rather than playhouses for the hearers, it is hardly to be wondered at if their managers and directors encourage those representations to which their structure is best adapted. The splendour of the scenes . . . now in a great degree supercede the labours of the poet. There can be nothing very gratifying in watching the movements of an actor's lips when we cannot hear the words that proceed from them, but when the animating march strikes up and the stage lays open its recesses to the depth of a hundred feet for the procession to advance, even the most distant spectator can enjoy his shilling's worth of show.'

By 1820 neither Drury Lane nor Covent Garden were doing much to justify their privileged positions. The former was administered by a committee of noble amateurs of whom Lord Byron was one. He reported that everyone argued with everyone else on matters of policy and that the play-reading sub-committee read about five hundred plays of which 'not one can be conscientiously tolerated.' From its declining fortunes Drury Lane was to be rescued, briefly, by the arrival of that flawed genius, Edmund Kean who, on 26 February 1814, made his startling debut at that theatre in the role of Shylock.

Kean's fame mounted rapidly. In quick succession he played Richard III, Hamlet, Othello, Iago and, in 1816, he persuaded Drury Lane to put on for him Massinger's *A New Way To Pay Old Debts* in which he played the villain Sir Giles Overreach. The sense of evil in his performance was so disturbing that many present at the first performance had to be removed in hysterics; Lord Byron had a convulsive fit, while many of Kean's fellow actors were terrified. Joseph Munden had to be dragged off stage by his armpits, murmuring 'My God, My God! Is it possible?'

In 1827, returned from America, he reappeared at Drury Lane in the role that had first made him famous. A great shout went up when he came on stage but his power and memory, the result of drink, had gone. He lay in bed at his hotel, drinking. He continued to flicker now and then. Several times he attempted a come-back. He appeared in a new play, *Ben Nazir* by Colley Grattan, but when he appeared on stage, he dried, improvised , and when the curtain fell on the first act, the manager had to come forward to make an apology. *Richard III* was magnificently got up for him but as the curtain was about to rise it was discovered that he was not in the house and it was days before he reappeared.

Now and then the town saw him but his hold on it was nearly gone. He was now at the Haymarket, and then uncertainly at Drury Lane, and again at the Haymarket in 1832, where he was seen for the last of many times as Richard. . . . 'The sight was pitiable,' wrote Dr Doran who was present. 'Genius was not traceable in that bloated face, intellect was all but quenched in those once matchless eyes, and the power seemed gone despite the will that would recall it. The end was at hand. To and from Richmond he occasionally travelled, a feeble bundle of humanity that seemed to lie unconsciously in one corner of his carriage. But, I think, conscience was there, too, and rage, and remorse—that a life had been so wasted, and . . . he aroused himself to make his last appearance, as it proved, on the stage, in conjunction with his son, as Othello, and Charles Kean, as Iago.

'By 25 March 1833, Edmund Kean was so shattered that he had scarcely strength to pass over him the dress of the Moor, so shattered in nerve that he dreaded some disaster. Brandy gave some little heart to the grossly fallen actor, but he anxiously enjoined his son to be ever near him in case of some mischance. And so he went through his part, dying as he went, till, after giving the sweet utterance, as of old, to the celebrated "Farewell," ending with "Othello's occupation's gone," he attempted to utter the next speech and in the attempt fell on his son's shoulder with a whispered moan, "I am dying. Speak to them for me." The curtain here descended on him for ever and the rest was only slow death with intervals of hope!' He died on 15 May 1833.

In 1819, Drury Lane had closed abruptly, with debts amounting to over £90,000. An advertisement appeared, inviting bids from prospective lessees, and on 8 September Robert William Elliston became the first autonomous manager the theatre had known since it was rebuilt.

Leigh Hunt, writing in 1807, had described Elliston as 'the greatest actor of the present day.' Physically he was best equipped for comedy and sustained his reputation as a comic actor until his death in 1831, but it was as an actor-manager that he was to make a lasting contribution to the repeal of the Licensing Act and the freeing of the Minor Theatres. In turn, and sometimes simultaneously, he was manager of the Royal Circus and the Olympic Pavilion, of Birmingham Theatre Royal, Drury Lane, and, finally, The Surrey. To quote Charles Lamb, 'Wherever Elliston walked, sate, or stood still, there was the theatre.'

On 18 February 1809, an advertisement appeared in *The Courier* announcing that the Trustees of The Royal Circus were inviting tenders for the lease. On 23 February Elliston signed a seven-year lease for the theatre. The Royal Circus, situated on the undeveloped south side of London, had been unlucky since its opening in 1782, and continually victimized by the Patent Theatres. Twice the actor John Palmer had been imprisoned for using dialogue. In 1805 it had been destroyed by fire and although it had been rebuilt it had been unable to compete with Astley's Amphitheatre, which was regarded as the only circus in London.

When Elliston took over in 1809, he not only presented the usual ballet, tightrope acrobatics and pantomime expected by audiences of the Royal Circus, but a production of *The Beggars Opera,* which he had ingeniously adapted into rhymed recitative with a musical accompaniment, and mimed action; and in this way it was able to qualify not as drama but as a burletta. It was an immediate success and marked the beginning of a whole style of presentation. It was followed by an adaptation of *Macbeth,* also as a burletta—'A Ballet of Music and Action' is how he described it. Apart from the use of mime, tableaux, rhymed recitative and songs, he also employed banners or scrolls on which were inscribed extracts from the play. This somewhat Brechtian device served to advance the action. Thus, after the departure of the witches in the first act, a messenger entered, bearing a banner inscribed, 'By Sinel's death, Macbeth is Thane of Glamis,' and shortly afterwards Macduff entered with a banner announcing 'Duncan doth create Macbeth Thane of Cawdor.' When Macbeth went to murder Duncan, a spirit sang the words 'Sleep no more, Macbeth doth murder sleep.'

The production was a mixture of mime, dance, opera and spectacle. There was a special *pas de trois* for the three witches, although he used sixteen witches for the coven scenes. Hecate descended from the clouds, while the ghost of Banquo ascended and descended, wreathed in clouds, through a trapdoor in the stage. Whether it was the result of this last effect or not, at one performance the audience called enthusiastically for Banquo, but the actor had gone home. The audience, however, was insistent on congratulating him in person, so a boy was dispatched to his home to bring him back to the theatre. When, finally, he appeared on the stage, in his own clothes, the audience fell silent, not recognizing him. Finally someone in the gallery called out, 'Who's that?' and was answered by a voice in the pit, 'Why, you fool, that's the author!'

As a manager, Elliston knew the importance of offering the audience comfortable and attractive surroundings, and in 1810 he spent £2,000 doing up the Royal Circus, and renaming it The Surrey Theatre. In place of the horse-ride was a large pit, while the stables were converted into elegant lounges, and the mangers into refreshment booths. There were also spacious coffee-rooms and foyers. There were chandeliers, crimson and gold draperies, an elaborate proscenium, and an ornamental ceiling painted with the story of Bacchus and Ariadne. It became, in time, one of the best known theatres in London, comfortable, with excellent acoustics and sight lines. Elliston was the first actor-manager to bring theatre to the suburbs. In 1811 he presented Garrick's play *Jubilee,* inserting into it seventeen mimed scenes from various Shakespeare plays, each scene being a miniature ballet. *The Times* wrote, 'Those worthy inhabitants of distant villages who from daily occupation and difference of habits, have hitherto had no time or inclination to peruse the works of our immortal bard, Shakespeare, have, on their coming to town, and paying a visit to The Surrey Theatre, imbibed, from the sample exhibited in the Grand Pageant, such a taste for Shakespearean productions, and so much curiosity to peruse plays, of which they have just seen enough to make them wish for more, that the demand for pocket editions and other sets of the Poet's works is so great, that the booksellers have of late been obliged to reprint them in all forms and sizes.'

Enraged by his success, the Patent Theatres tried to have the Royal Circus closed down but Elliston waged a successful battle against them over the precise definition of 'burletta.' He now named the theatre, the Olympic New Theatre, and in 1818 staged productions with established actors and elaborate scenery, deliberately challenging the major theatres. He also included in that season's programme a three-act burletta, *Rochester,* which abandoned a musical introduction to each scene and can therefore claim to be the first regular drama produced at a minor theatre without an accompanying tinkle of the piano.

It was in the following year that Elliston achieved his ambition of becoming manager of a major theatre when, on 8 September 1819, he became manager of Drury Lane. He at once sacked unnecessary and parasitic staff (some forty were struck off the payroll) and he became the first manager to issue contracts to actors. Like Garrick he insisted on punctuality, conscientious work, and good manners both on and back stage, and instituted a new set of fines for all theatre staff. Realizing the dearth of new drama, he tried to commission plays from the best writers. Sir Walter Scott and Thomas Moore declined. (In 1819, writing to a friend, Sir Walter Scott observed 'I do not think the character of the audience in London is such that one could have the least pleasure in pleasing them. One half come to prosecute their debaucheries so openly that it would disgrace a bagnio; another set to snooze off their beefsteaks and port wine; a third are critics of the fourth column of the newspaper; fashion, wit or literature there is not.') And although he received scripts from Keats, Shelley and Leigh Hunt, they proved unsuitable for the stage. Byron had left England and it was to be a year before he wrote his first stage play.

Thus, at the outset of his management, Elliston was faced with the recurring problem of Regency theatre: the lack of good dramatists. It is interesting to observe that in his diary for 1806, George Frederick Cooke, the actor, had written, 'There are a damned set of writers at the present day.' Cooke, as J. C. Trewin records in *The Pomping Folk,* 'glowers at us from British theatre history as if expecting trouble. In life he had plenty of it; quarrelsome and intemperate, he seems to loom across the stage of his period, a glass permanently in his hand. Again and again, in London and elsewhere, he failed to appear when announced, or had—among angry heckling—to apologise for inability to proceed: "Ladies and gentlemen—my old complaint—my old complaint!" '

At Covent Garden, during June 1810, as Falstaff in *Henry IV, Part I,* he spoke his last words in the London Theatre, 'I'll purge, and leave sack, and live cleanly as a nobleman should do.' That autumn he was in New York, and he remained in America until his death in 1812.

On 30 January 1820 King George III died. On 19 July, on the occasion of the coronation of George IV, Elliston presented at Drury Lane a fascimile representation of the occasion. For ninety minutes the audience witnessed on the stage of Drury Lane the procession to the Abbey, the ceremony within, and the banquet that followed. It was all staged with such complete accuracy that when Elliston entered as George IV (to whom in real life he bore a marked resemblance) the audience rose to its feet, cheering. Some idea of the splendour of the spectacle can be seen in the toy theatre prints issued for the occasion by the printer West.

In 1822 Elliston gutted the inside of the building, rebuilt it, making many improvements that were aimed at attracting a more middle-class audience. He also brought the stage closer to the audience. With its reopening he began to pay enormous salaries in order to secure top star performers in an effort to rival Covent Garden. One of his greatest triumphs was *The Cataract of the Ganges,* the huge success of which illustrates the direction in which drama was moving. This melodrama began with a scene (designed by Clarkson Stanfield) set in a Hindu temple, with a bridal procession that included a carriage drawn by six horses, two military bands, soldiers carrying banners, and troupes of slaves and dancing girls. The finale involved, amidst a full-scale military battle, an exit on horseback through a cataract, surrounded by blazing fire. *The London Magazine* considered the cataract 'something like the pouring of a good teapot, only flatter; it was in truth no broader than a yard of sixpenny ribbon . . . we ourselves could have walked up the fall in pumps and not have wetted the upper leathers,' while *The Morning Chronicle* prophesied with remarkable accuracy) that if *The Cataract* succeeded, it was farewell to Shakespeare 'and welcome noise and nonsense, and all the tinsel and trumpery with their splendid delusions, to gratify the grown children of the metropolis!'

Elliston succeeded in clearing the debts of Drury Lane but, as was to be found repeatedly, the strain of managing such a huge theatre, proved insupportable. He collapsed with a stroke. In 1827, having recovered, he returned once more to act and manage The Surrey Theatre. A review of his particularly fine performance as Falstaff is worth quoting in that it reveals another important aspect of the minor theatres in the development of a new style of acting. The smaller size of the theatre,' observed *The Weekly Dramatic Register,*' enables us to perceive all the minute and elaborate beauties of Mr Elliston's acting: the smile trickles from the mouth and eye perceptibly, however unformed and unexaggerated . . . we are delivered from those conventional signs which the larger theatres force upon the actors . . . . The voice, too, may be heard in its own key, and avail itself of the richness and depth of the lower tones without the forced expedient of an artificial loudness.'

As Christopher Murray has observed in his definitive study, *Robert William Elliston–Manager,* Elliston's contribution to the movement that finally led, in 1843, to the formal revoking of the Monopoly Laws, was perhaps greater than that of anyone else. He it was who initiated the establishment of the minor theatres as places where self-respecting actors and authors might find an outlet for their talents. He it was who proved that these places could achieve and maintain artistic standards. By so doing, he had given the playwrights and actors a stake in the minor theatres, so that the question of monopoly came to be seen as central to the future of English dramatic literature.

21.   Typical entertainment at Sadler's Wells in 1822—African Sal and Dusty Bob.

22.   The interior of Sadler's Wells, 1809.

23.　The burning of Covent Garden Theatre, 12 September 1808.

24.   Thomas Rowlandson's illustration of John Bull at the Italian Opera.

25.   The Old Price Riots at Covent Garden, when for fifty nights the audience rioted and protested against the new prices charged by the new theatre.

26.   The Surrey Theatre, 1812. Originally the Royal Circus, this theatre was taken over in 1809 by the enterprising manager R. W. Elliston, who spent £2,000 renovating it.

27.   The Olympic Theatre in 1831.

28. Astley's Amphitheatre in 1808. Astley's was the popular home of equestrian melodramas and displays, much loved by Dickens and described in *The Old Curiosity Shop*.

29. For the coronation of King George IV in 1820, Elliston staged at Drury Lane a reproduction of the ceremony, including the procession to the Abbey, the ceremony inside and the banquet which followed.

30.   John Opie's portrait of Master Betty in the role of Young Norval.

MR GRIMALDI AS CLOWN.

P.Five Halfpenny.

ILLUMINATING THE ENTRANCE TO OLD GUTTER LANE.

31. Portrait of Joseph Grimaldi, the much loved clown of the nineteenth century and one of the great figures in the history of London's theatre.

32.   Poster for a Grimaldi benefit—between 1806 and 1828 Grimaldi transformed the knockabout entertainment of pantomime into a vehicle for the most sophisticated satire.

33.   The great and tragic actor Edmund Kean as Sir Giles Overreach in *A New Way to Pay Old Debts*.

34. The dress circle at a London theatre: from the 1860s onwards, the middle classes were slowly lured back to the theatres, but at the cost of driving out the lower classes who began to frequent the music halls.

35. Children at a special performance at the Royal Victorian Coffee Hall (the Old Vic) in 1882.

London Published by W. S. Fores 50 Piccadilly Augt 9th 1817

*May I die if there is'nt Sir George !!
— charming man !! as I live he's looking
this way — O! the dear fellow !! Vide the Opera boxes*

36.   'A show is not a show but they that go . . .'. A young lady in a box at the theatre, 1817.

37.   Saturday night at the Victoria Theatre (the Old Vic). The Vic became a
favourite resort of a young, rowdy and huge audience.

39. The Panopticon Music hall.

38. 'It was, I think . . . the capacity for expressing the soul of the people that made Marie Lloyd unique and that made her audience . . . not so much hilarious as happy,' wrote T. S. Eliot.

40.   Aerial effects, including flights out over the audience, were especially popular, as in Kellar's sensational levitation act, 'from stage to dome'.

Chapter six

The Nineteenth Century: II

Grimaldi·Macready·three cheers for Phelps·the penny gaff·Marie Lloyd·prudes on the prowl

The pantomime had been a major dramatic form in London theatre for decades before the appearance, in 1806, at Covent Garden (via Sadlers Wells) of an artist whose genius was to transform a spectacular knockabout form of entertainment, dominated by the character of harlequin, into a vehicle for satire, dominated instead by the clown. From 1806 until 1823, when he was forced prematurely to retire because of illness, Joseph Grimaldi was hailed as the greatest clown of the British pantomime, creating the type of clown still known as 'Joey'. Under his influence the pantomime became, as Leigh Hunt described it in 1817, 'at present the best medium of dramatic literature.' Strictly an entertainment for adults, it became as topically allusive as did, at a later period, the revue. The invention of steam boats, of coaches, of gas for illumination, the evolution of commerce, voyages by balloon, the dilemma of the poor, the extremes of fashion and, especially, of dandyism, were all targets for the scathing wit of Grimaldi, who once said, 'It's all in my way, you know. I play the fool to show others the absurdity of it.' As another contemporary critic wrote, 'Pantomime forms a powerful engine . . . for striking sharply and rapidly at the monstrosities of time.'

Joey the clown was an acrobat, a juggler, a swordsman, a dancer, a singer, a mime. He could design and paint scenery, make props, arrange stage fights and choreograph dances. He also loved to garden, make shoes, do carpentry, invent conjuring tricks, play the violin, keep pigeons, and collect butterflies. He would invent fantastic visual stage tricks, creating a man out of vegetables from the market, or make a chariot from a cradle, with circular cheeses as wheels, drawn by dogs. On stage he commanded a far wider technical range than any modern comic. He would stand, looking out at the vast, candle-lit, audience, with 'a thousand odd twitches and unaccountable absurdities oozing out at every pore' of his clownish mask. His eyebrows would go up 'like a pair of umbrellas, or one would ascend and the other remain to superintend the wink.' His chin was unusually mobile; he could lower it suddenly with an alarming drop. His oven-mouth was enough to convulse the audience. 'Every limb of him had a language.'

In spite of his success, however, Grimaldi experienced many difficulties and disappointments. When his London home was burgled, and his prize collection of butterflies stolen, he was to experience the first of many losses. He was to lose his wife, his son, his beloved garden, his pigeons, and be forced, through ill health, to retire early from the stage. At the end he was completely alone, and his limbs so crippled that he had to be carried on the shoulders of a friend whenever he went out.

On Friday, 27 June 1828, Grimaldi gave his farewell performance at Drury Lane Theatre. He played only one short scene, seated on a chair. At the end he reappeared in his everyday clothes and 'his entry was the signal for a shout loud enough to rend the roof,' wrote the *New Monthly Magazine*. 'He stood up, his knees tottering and every feature of his face convulsed . . . Mr Harley attempted to run on to assist him, but was restrained by young Grimaldi, who knew that his father had taxed his energies for a last effort, and that those energies would not desert him.

' "Ladies and gentlemen," began Grimaldi, "I appear before you for the last time. I need not assure you of the sad regret with which I say it, but sickness and infirmity have come upon me and I can no longer wear the motley. Four years ago I jumped my last jump, filched my last oyster and ate my last sausage. I cannot describe the pleasure I felt on once more assuming my cap and bells tonight—that dress in which I have so often been made happy in your applause; and as I stripped them off, I fancied that they seemed to cleave to me. I am not so rich a man as I was when I was basking in your favour formerly, for then I had always a fowl in one pocket and sauce for it in the other. I thank you for the benevolence which has brought you here to assist your old and faithful servant in his premature decline. Eight and forty years have not yet passed over my head, and I am sinking fast. I now stand worse upon my legs than I used to do on my head. But, I suppose I am paying the penalty of the course I pursued all my life; my desire and anxiety to merit your favour has excited me to more exertion than my constitution could bear, and, like vaulting ambition, I have over-leaped myself. Ladies and gentlemen, I must hasten to bid you farewell; but the pain I feel in doing so is assuaged by seeing before me a disproof of the old adage, that favourites have no friends. Ladies and gentlemen, may you and yours enjoy the blessings of health is the fervent prayer of Joseph Grimaldi. Farewell! Farewell!" '

At the end, Grimaldi stood on the stage, swaying before the footlights, tears running down his cheeks as the audience roared their applause, thundering the floor with their feet, banging the benches, and throwing their hats into the air. Wave after wave of applause exploded from the thousands of people who wanted to express their gratitude to the man who, for so many years, had given them so much happiness and gaiety.

The streets outside were thronged with people waiting to see him emerge and, as he entered his coach which stood at the stage door, they gave him three cheers. Hundreds followed the carriage until it reached his house and, upon being helped out, he was once again hailed by shouts of 'Joey! Good old Joey! Joey the clown!'

The only other farewell performance that matched it in this century was that of William Charles Macready, the eminent tragedian, at Drury Lane on 26 February 1851. Thousands gathered in the rain to say farewell to Macready who, for thirty years, had been the leading tragic actor of the London theatre. Three thousand people, and not a few pickpockets, were crowded outside the theatre at 6.30 p.m., and every window overlooking Drury Lane was packed.

At his first entrance onto the stage as Macbeth—his most famous role—the whole house rose to its feet, waving hats and handkerchiefs, roaring with such a frenzy and excitement that George Henry Lewes, looking down from his box, wondered whether the actor would be able to continue. 'What a sight!' he wrote afterwards, 'how glorious, triumphant, affecting!'

Successor to Burbage, Betterton, Garrick, John Philip Kemble and Edmund Kean, Macready was a great actor who never really wanted to be an actor. He strove to redeem the theatre of its many blatancies, to create a home worthy of national drama, and to restore many of the Shakespeare texts. He appeared upon the scene when drama was perhaps at its lowest ebb. In 1833, the notorious Alfred Bunn was trying to manage Drury Lane and Covent Garden simultaneously. He expected players to act in the opening piece at Covent Garden (where opera and ballet predominated) and then to scurry through the winter darkness, across Bow Street, in order to act in the afterpiece at Drury Lane.

'As for the "patent movable company",' wrote John Bull on 13 December 1833, 'the two houses, under the present system, incur but one expense—no matter where they are—now at the "Lane," now at the "Garden." We are told that at certain periods of the evening, it is quite curious to see the actors and actresses running, hurry-scurry, skimble-skamble, from one house to the other—the Drury Lane Romeo rushing up to Market Court in his black puffs and bugles, to act Sir Christopher Curry at Covent Garden, bumping himself full butt at the corner, against the Covent Garden Jaffeir, scudding before the breeze to play Dr Pangloss at Drury Lane; and then the ladies, slip-slops, spangles and sandals, rain or blow, hail or snow, away they go, Peruvian virgins . . . at full tilt, to become Witches on Macbeth's heath, well secured against the weather by pattens and plaid cloaks . . . how far this system of economy will work well, as regards the health of the "labourers" it is impossible to say, especially when the sharp weather sets in. It is quite wonderful that so few delays take place and that so little interruption occurs to the performances thus carried on.'

By 1835 there were no less than fifteen minor theatres in existence, strenuously fighting to get Parliament to repeal the strangling legislation that upheld the monopoly of the two patented houses. Of the many factors that strengthened their case was the apparent failure of anyone to be able to make either Drury Lane or Covent Garden function as theatres for legitimate drama. They were, clearly, too large. In 1837, however, Macready made a last attempt to salvage both Covent Garden and, from 1841 until 1843, Drury Lane. In 1843 the Patent Theatres' monopoly was abolished.

Macready was the first theatre director, in the modern sense of the word. Until then, there was almost no attempt to fit characterizations together, to concentrate on the development of scenes, and to relate these to the overall rhythm of the play. In his early days Macready had often been laughed at for acting in rehearsal, and when he became a manager, he applied this principle to every actor, rehearsing the extras with the same care that he rehearsed the leading actors. An entire morning would be devoted to the extras in *King John*. His prompt copy for *As You Like It* (in the Folger Shakespeare Library) reveals the Stanislavsky-like detail of his productions, the orchestration of the stage picture from moment to moment.

Like Stanislavsky, he was also one of the first actors to stress the importance of inner realism. 'The highest reach of the player's art,' he wrote, 'is to fathom the depths of the character, to trace its latent motives, to feel its finest quiverings of emotion, to comprehend the thoughts that are hidden under words and thus possess oneself of the actual mind of the individual.'

The great American actor, Joseph Jefferson, recalled that Macready always began to assume his character the moment he entered the theatre. He would remain in his dressing-room, absorbing himself in the part, with his dresser stationed just outside the door, ready to open it just before he was due on stage.

'My long experience of the stage,' wrote Macready, 'has convinced me of the necessity of keeping, on the day of the exhibition, the mind as intent as possible on the subject of the actor's portraiture, even to the very moment of his entrance upon the scene. He meditates himself, as it were, into the very thought and feeling of the person he is about to represent.'

J. C. Trewin, in his moving study of the actor, *Mr Macready*, cites the most famous example of Macready's concentration on the character when, as Shylock, before the Tubal scene, 'he worked himself into a violent passion before his entry by seizing the ladder to the flies, shaking it, and uttering language that made the stage hands stare at his latest eccentricity.' As a young actor I used to witness the Shakespearean actor, Donald Wolfit, do the same thing before going on stage in *Othello* for the fit scene.

Macready kept a detailed journal, analysing each of his own performances as well as those of other actors. These journals, like his letters, are as absorbing and as important a record of the craft of acting as the writings of the Russian, Constantin Stanislavsky who, in many ways, he anticipated. In a letter written to a friend, John Forster, who had asked Macready for help in an amateur production of *Every Man In His Humour* (the production in which Charles Dickens played Bobadil) Macready sends a detailed description of the kind of costume and properties that the character of Kitely would be likely to use.

'Kitely should always wear his keys. His hair is cropped—see print. The girdle is the cord around his waist. The sword of Kitely is a *real* Toledo—just such a one as such respectable gentlemen would have worn . . . but you had better look at T. Gresham's statue or print—or ask my sister to show it to you in the second volume of costumes in my dressing-room, in which you will see the habit of an English merchant in Elizabeth's reign, which will give you all the information. The hook is for his keys—a large bunch; his watch should be on a small fob on the right side. . . . He should wear his sword, or put it on, in the Counting House scene with the Cash . . . perhaps it would be very good if in his second scene, his sword, hat, and gloves were lying together on the table, and he were to hook on his sword as he takes it with his gloves etc, on the stage. *I could turn that to account.*'

The influence of Macready's ideas, example and acting practice, upon the younger generation of actors, both in England and America, is incalculable, as the late Professor Alan Downer has remarked. Of his own company, a young actor called Samuel Phelps was to reap much of the harvest sown by Macready through his work at Sadler's Wells.

When Macready took over Drury Lane in 1842 the Press looked to him as the last hope of the British theatre. Increasingly, however, he found that the strains of being manager, director and leading actor, were intolerable, and affecting his own performances. 'I am falling off in my art through my attention to management,' he wrote at one point, and, later, 'Whirled along as I now am in the current of harassing and irritating business I have little opportunity for reflection.' Henry Irving, likewise, was to feel the same and Ellen Terry records that, almost invariably, Irving gave his least good performances on his opening nights.

'Thine is it that our drama did not die,' wrote the Poet Laureate, Tennyson, on the retirement of Macready:

> 'Nor flicker down to brainless pantomime
> And those gilt-gauds men-children swarm to see.'

At the Princess Theatre, from 1851 to 1859, Charles Kean staged a series of productions, mainly of Shakespeare, in which, as he ponderously expressed it, 'historical accuracy might be so blended with pictorial effect that instruction and amusement would go hand in hand.' Until then, productions had been, in the main, a mixture of styles and periods, without any connection with the historical context of a drama, Macready being the outstanding exception. The Victoria and Albert Museum possesses a unique collection of watercolour sketches showing Kean's major productions and there is no doubt that both Henry Irving and Beerbohm Tree were influenced by Kean's methods of staging. He engaged scholars and antiquarians to advise on, and artists to paint, the sets. His *Henry VIII* was an especial success with the public. For this, Grieve used a diorama. An immensely long cloth, representing the entire length of the Thames, was stretched between two rollers, which revolved in unison, so that, as the actor playing Henry stood motionless on the barge, the audience had the illusion of the barge sailing upstream.

For *A Midsummer Night's Dream* he recreated the world of classical Greece—although the effect was somewhat ruined by Mrs Kean insisting on wearing a crinoline under her 'real' Greek robe. Kean's production of *The Merchant of Venice* attempted to recreate sixteenth-century Venice. He often employed as many as five hundred people on a production, and on one season alone spent a sum little short of £50,000. The Cecil B. de Mille of the Victorian theatre, he was frequently satirized in the press. For example, on 8 November 1856, *Punch* inserted the following notice:

> 'The alligator who is said to be the grand star of the Zoological Gardens next season has already been engaged for the Princess Theatre. It is to make its first appearance on the banks of the Nile in *Antony and Cleopatra* which is to be revived for the occasion on a most enormous scale of splendour.'

It is easy to mock the productions of Charles Kean, Irving and Tree, but they brought people back to the theatre, many of whom were discovering Shakespeare for the first time. Tree was constantly being criticized for the lavishness of his productions (real animals, real buildings, grass and water and trees and vegetation) but, as he remarked, 'Shakespeare scholars say I'm wrong in tempting people to come to the theatre and giving them a spectacle instead of Shakespeare. But I prefer spectacles on the stage to spectacles in the audience!'

The renaissance of Shakespeare as a playwright, and the unceasing variety of interpretations that mark the twentieth century, take their roots from the productions of Macready, Kean, Irving, Tree—and Samuel Phelps.

Perhaps the toughest task tackled by any manager in the London theatre of the nineteenth century (with the exception of the Old Vic) was that at Sadler's Wells when it was taken over in 1844 by Samuel Phelps and Mary Warner. Dickens, writing in 1851, recalled, 'seven or eight years ago this theatre was in the condition of being entirely delivered over to as ruffianly an audience as London could shake together. Without, the theatre by night was the worst of the worst kind of fair in the worst kind of town. Within, it was a bear garden, resounding with foul language, oaths, catcalls, shrieks, yells, blasphemy, obscenity—a truly diabolical clamour. Fights, too, took place anywhere at any period of the performance.'

The fair, held nightly outside the theatre and patronized by thieves and prostitutes, discouraged the more respectable from attending the theatre. Immediately upon taking over, Phelps ordered the various showmen, the proprietors of shooting galleries, exhibitors of freaks, etc, off the premises. In consequence, when Phelps opened with *Macbeth,* they took their revenge, and that first performance was held 'amidst the usual hideous medley of fights, foul language, catcalls, shrieks, yells, oaths, blasphemy, obscenity, apples oranges, nuts, biscuits, ginger beer, porter and pipes—pipes of every description were at work in the gallery and in the pit. Cans of beer .... were carried through the dense crowd at all stages of the tragedy. Sickly children in arms were squeezed out of shape in all parts of the house. Fish was fried at the entrance doors. Barricades of oyster shells encumbered the pavement.'

There is a story that, after the first act, Phelps in his costume as Macbeth, having spotted the ringleader from the stage, appeared suddenly in the gallery and hauled him out amidst a cry of 'Three cheers for Phelps!'

However, even when, eventually, he did succeed in training the Wells audience to be attentive, he still had to put up with the pittites, crowded up to the stage on their benches, drinking ginger beer or stout, sucking oranges, cracking nuts, and crunching apples. 'The friers of fish, vendors of oysters, and other costermonger scum' accumulated around the doors, were the first to go. The noisy sellers of beer inside the theatre were the next to be removed. They resisted and offered a large weekly consideration 'for leave to sell a call.' The management was obdurate and rooted them out. Children in arms were next to be expelled. Orders were given to the money-takers to refuse them admission, but these were found to be extremely difficult to be enforced, as 'the women smuggled babies in under their shawls, aprons, and even rolled them up to look like cloaks. A little experience of such artifices led to their detection at the doors and the play soon began to go without the shrill interruptions consequent on the unrolling of dozens of these unfortunate little mummies every night.'

In order to combat the use of foul language, Phelps found a disused Act of Parliament under which the use of such language in a public place was subject to a fine 'and it was enforced with such vigour that on several occasions Mr Phelps stopped the play to have the offender removed.'

Phelps presented not only thirty-one of Shakespeare's thirty-four plays in eighteen years, but he also produced seventy-one other classic plays, as well as eleven new dramas—an average of over eight new productions a year. He made of Sadler's Wells what the Old Vic would become a century later. He restored in the original texts three plays of Shakespeare seen since the Restoration only in adapted form: *Richard III, Antony and Cleopatra, Timon of Athens.* From *King Lear, Romeo and Juliet* and *Macbeth,* he removed the last remnants of adaptation; in seven plays he discarded acting texts for the originals, and he brought to the stage in Shakespeare's text four other plays, acted seldom since the closing of the theatres in 1642, including that rarity, *Pericles.* The success of Phelps's management of Sadler's Wells from 1844 until 1862 demonstrated for the first time that the classic repertory of the English stage could attract and hold a popular audience. After a few seasons his inexperienced audience became known for its discriminating appreciation and for a remarkable acquaintance with poetic drama. The productions began to attract theatregoers from other parts of London—*Punch* goaded the Queen on several occasions for not visiting the theatre in Islington.

The Morning Advertiser, in 1855–6, noting how attentive were the audiences, said 'whoever desires to see the true uses of the stage, and the value of a national drama, be he scholar or unlearned, high or low, should certainly wend his way to Sadler's Wells.' By this time, the Wells was coming to be regarded as an example to other London theatres. It was about now that in the audiences at the Wells were the young Squire Bancroft, and Irving, then aged eighteen. Henry Morley, writing in 1853, observed, 'There sit the working-classes in a happy crowd, as orderly and reverent as if they were in church, and yet as unrestrained in their enjoyment as if listening to stories told to them by their own firesides. *A Midsummer Night's Dream* abounds in the most delicate of Shakespeare's verse; the Sadler's Wells pit has a keen enjoyment of them, and the pit and gallery were crowded to the farthest wall on Saturday night with a most earnest audience, among whom many a subdued hush arose, not during but just before the delivery of the most charming passages. If the crowd at Drury Lane is a gross discredit to public taste, the crowd at Sadler's Wells more than neutralise any ill opinion that may on that score be formed of playgoers.'

Some of Phelps's productions were staged simply, some ambitiously. From Macready he had learned, among many things, how to handle crowds on stage. Thus, in 1848, so excited was the audience on one occasion that, after the usual curtain for the leading actors, the cry of 'Supers!' was heard. 'By God!' said Phelps, grinning, 'they are calling for the supers! And, demme, they deserve it. Never seen better acting in my life!' The curtains opened and the crowd of extras was duly cheered.

His production of *Henry V,* though not as visually elaborate as Macready's famous version, had one ingenious piece of stagecraft. For the march-past before Agincourt, he had his forty supers filing behind a chest-high rock. Each soldier had strapped to his body two wicker-work dummies in armour, the heads modelled specially by Madame Tussaud, so that the soldiers appeared to be marching three abreast. As they tramped past, banners streaming, drums beating, trumpets braying, the stage seemed crowded with soldiers and the illusion was so perfect that the audience never once discovered how it was done.

When, in 1862, Phelps retired, the Wells went into decline, as is so often the way with theatres and churches, the size of audience or congregation being dependent upon the personality, vision and talents of the incumbent. In the succeeding years, various managers took over the theatre. Melodramas were presented, a female Hamlet, even a *Macbeth* with a different Macbeth for each act. The young Arthur Pinero took an active part in complaining from the pit about the slovenly condition of the theatre, and was rebuked from the stage as 'the boy in the scotch cap.'

In 1874 it was wound up as a theatre and in 1876 converted into a skating rink. This enterprise failed as also did The Actors' Cooperative Society in 1889. No manager since Phelps appeared able to find a successful policy and, until the turn of the century, it became, under George Belmont, a Variety house, nicknamed 'Sunny Old Sad's.'

Just as the growing class-consciousness of the new middle-classes was reflected in their challenge to the established privilege of the Patent Houses, and in the founding of more Minor Theatres, so the growing working-class consciousness was reflected in the development of Saloon Theatres, penny gaffs, and other illegal theatres from the 1820s onward. The Saloon Theatres were mainly aggrandized public houses where patrons could join in a sing-song or be entertained over drinks by visiting artists. Among the most popular of the Saloon Theatres were: The Grecian or Eagle Tavern in the City Road; The Canterbury Arms in Lambeth, and The Britannia at Hoxton.

The gaff was, literally, theatre for a penny. The penny gaff was usually a converted shop, and performances began when enough people had been assembled. On an average there would be about six performances an evening. The audience, mainly aged between eight and twenty, sat on benches for an entertainment that consisted of sketches, farces, songs and drag acts. Blanchard Jerrold in *London: A Pilgrimage*, illustrated by Doré, describes a penny gaff:

'The true penny gaff is the place where juvenile poverty meets juvenile crime. We elbowed our way into one that was the foulest, dingiest place of public entertainment I can conceive; and I have seen, I think, the worst in many places. The narrow passages were blocked by sharp-eyed young thieves . . . a platform, with bedaubed proscenium, was the stage, and the boxes were as dirty as the stalls of a common stable. The odour—the atmosphere—to begin with, is indescribable. The rows of brazen young faces are terrible to look upon.'

Jerrold and Doré find a trio singing as they arrive, 'accompanying the searing words with mimes and gestures, and hinted indecencies that are immensely relished. The boys and girls nod to each other and laugh aloud: they have understood. Not a wink has been lost upon them.'

Yet the penny gaffs, like the music halls, provided an important creative outlet: by poking fun at the everyday disasters of life, they helped to set them in perspective. 'Mr S reproaches Mrs S with the possession of a private bottle of gin,' records the journalist Augustus Sala of one entertainment. 'Mrs S inveighs against the hideous turpitude of Mr S for pawning three pillow cases to purchase beer. The audiences are in ecstasies. It is *so* real.'

Henry Mayhew, writing at the end of the 1840s, describes how the costermongers around the New Cut at Waterloo and Blackfriars Road used regularly to visit the theatres on an average of three times a week. 'Love and murder suits us best, sir,' says one, 'but within these few years I think there's a great deal more liking for deep tragedies among us. They set men a-thinking, but then we consider they all go on too long.'

Mayhew describes such an audience at The Old Victoria in the New Cut, in *London Labour and the London Poor*, published in 1851. 'That house became a favourite resort of a huge and rowdy audience fed with farces, melodramas, songs, and dancing.'—Entrance to 'the gods' cost three pence and the long staircase leading up to their tumultuous heaven was crowded with costers before the opening. 'It was a young audience . . . chiefly composed of lads and girls and young mothers with their babies (the infants, poor wretches, got in for a penny halfpenny) and it was a hungry one too. The ham-sandwich men and pig-trotter women did a brisk trade all night and there was much throwing of orange peel and nutshells.'

'In the gallery,' wrote Hollingshead, 'were 1500 perspiring creatures, bare-headed, in shirt sleeves. This chickaleary audience was always thirsty and not ashamed. They would tie up their handkerchiefs together and haul up bottles of beer from the pit. Their likes and dislikes were made deafeningly evident.' At the back, we learn, there were also 'piles of boys on each others' shoulders.'

Theatre-going was an essential part of the working-class way of life. Although legally limited to burlettas until 1843, the audiences of the Minor Theatres longed for legitimate drama and John Hollingshead remembers actors from Mrs Harwood's penny gaff being marched through the streets of Shoreditch, in the costumes of *Othello*, with eighty members of the audience, to Worship Street Police Station.

When Sam Lane lost his licence at The Britannia in Hoxton for staging a straight production of *Black Eyed Susan,* he led a procession to Westminster with East Enders waving banners, proclaiming 'Workers Want Theatres!' When Edward Bulwer came to campaign in Parliament in the 1830s for the ending of the Theatres' Patents Act, he was strongly backed by these Minor Theatres.

When finally in 1843 the new Theatres Act was passed, one of the first, now legal, Minor Theatres to present plays was The Brit—as it was affectionately called (in much the same way that the Royal Victoria was to become known, with equal affection, as the Old Vic). Sam Lane told his audience, 'I am proud to have helped in this success in obtaining freedom for the people's amusement. Never again will you be deprived of free theatre.'

The Brit was, in many ways, unique. When it was rebuilt in 1858 Dickens wrote, 'I was in an immense theatre, capable of holding 5000. His Majesty's? Royal Italian opera? Infinitely superior to the latter for hearing, infinitely superior to both for seeing in.' The Brit also helped to pioneer Shakespeare for the working-class audience. Ira Aldridge, the famous American negro actor, played both his Othello, and Aaron (*Titus Andronicus*) there in 1852.

During the 1830s, the rapid development of public transport resulted in a redistribution of the population of central London, causing the more well-to-do families to move out to Greenwich, Highgate and Stockwell. It is this shift of population that in part explains why, in spite of the continuing rise of population, no theatres were built in Central London and Westminster between 1840 and 1867. One of the other main reasons for the exodus from central London of middle-class families was the rapidly deteriorating standard of living conditions in the capital. An article appearing in *The Morning Chronicle* in September 1849 described London as 'the very capital of cholera.' Charles Kingsley visited 'the cholera districts of Bermondsey' in 1849 and related that he saw people 'with no water to drink but that of the common sewer stagnating under their windows, full of dead fish, cats and dogs.' It was not only in the poorer districts that sanitation was either wholly absent or totally ineffective. During the early part of Queen Victoria's reign, a sewer was allowed to run into the Serpentine, whose waters were fouled. Gases emerged which caused fevers to spread. It was not until 1860 that the sewage was diverted. Early Victorian London had far more earth closets and cesspools than water-closets connected with main drainage. It is perhaps worth noting that there were no public lavatories until those installed at the Crystal Palace in 1854. How people managed during the long programmes of the eighteenth and nineteenth centuries seems not to be recorded, not even by such observers as Pepys or Boswell who, in such matters, might not be considered fastidious. Even when a Bill was passed commanding the provision of a water-closet in every house instead of the usual cesspool outside it, the early Victorian sewers still continued to discharge their contents into the Thames. In 1849, 18,000 people died from cholera, and in 1854, another 20,000. Yet in 1853, the private water companies were still supplying drinking water from the Thames for their customers.

Engels, writing in 1844, observed how, even in the immediate neighbourhood of Drury Lane Theatre, 'there are some of the worst streets in the whole metropolis—Charles Street, King Street, Park Street—in which the houses are inhabited from cellar to garret exclusively by poor families.' This overcrowding of London is a recurring feature of many children's books of the period. Standing immediately to the west of the Patent Theatres were the two worst 'rookeries' in London—St Giles and Seven Dials, described by Dickens as the worst area in London. From 1830 to 1831 Drury Lane suffered from outbreaks of cholera, while prostitutes, beggars and criminals haunted these streets by night. It is little wonder that, as one visitor to London remarked, 'the higher and more civilized classes go only to the Italian Opera [in the well-lit Haymarket] and very rarely visit their national theatre.'

Because the large, rowdy audiences of the early nineteenth century alienated the more sophisticated playgoers as much as the neighbourhood squalor and the danger of pickpockets, enterprising managers began to try and win them back by improving conditions. When Macready took over Drury Lane in 1837, one of his first acts was to exclude 'the women of the town' from the two lowest tiers of boxes. He also cleaned up the place so that when the audience arrived on the opening night they found that 'the festoons of richest cobwebs' on the ceiling had given way to an azure blue, while the walls were painted in a light vermilion, and the boxes in white and gold. Cushions that had been stained with tobacco, porter and 'other noxious filth' had been recovered and the pit benches provided with back rests.

Charles Kean at the Princess's Theatre in the 1850s drilled his box-keepers until they were able to open and close the doors of the boxes 'with the most preternatural quietness.' He even advertised that 'all the policemen selected for duty are members of the Church of England, while the estimable and accomplished linkman is a distinguished Anabaptist.'

In 1869, Mrs John Wood at the St James's Theatre, abolished the pit, replacing the backless benches with stalls seats. She inaugurated a rule of no tipping, and no charges for cloakrooms or programmes. The latter included reprints of press reviews, details of items lost and found in the theatre: 'Lady's golosh, lorgnette case, three umbrellas, walking cane, shawl, cigar-holder, smelling-bottle, pen-knife, lady's bag, brooch, muff. . . .' The back page included details of cab and railway fares, the various omnibus routes, and price of refreshments. In 1879, when the actor John Hare took over the theatre, the foyer was turned into a gallery, as an additional attraction, displaying paintings by Corot, Alma Tadema, G. F. Watts, and others. A new type of middle-class theatre, from the St James's to the Prince of Wales's Theatre (under the Bancrofts) began to emerge. It reached its quintessence under George Alexander and is perfectly described by Margaret Webster, whose mother, May Whitty, was a member of Alexander's company at the St James's in the 1890s. 'Everything was in place from the very first rehearsal. The departmental heads were like beneficent butlers . . . the housekeeper, Mrs Evans, ruled backstage with an iron hand. . . . There would be tea in the Green Room on matinée days, cake and sandwiches and a silver tea-service. Everything was conducted with the utmost decorum, and there were separate staircases for the ladies' and gentlemen's dressing rooms. It was the Establishment theatre *par excellence*. Here the feudal system worked to perfection.'

When the Bancrofts introduced the ten-shilling stall at the Prince of Wales Theatre in 1874, it was in order to pay for higher salaries, royalties to authors (something that, until then, had not existed) and greater comfort for audience and actors alike. Above all, they helped to raise the prestige of playgoing, to bring back the middle-classes to the theatre, but at the cost of driving out the working-classes who, increasingly now, began to frequent the music halls instead. During the 1860s the number of such halls in London increased rapidly.

It was also a period of acute economic discontent and this found its outlet for the working-classes in many of the songs heard in the music halls:

> The newspapers are all my eye,
> So don't the Times or Sun peruse;
> Just listen to me and I'll try
> To tell you what's the daily news.
> The daily news is this, my boys—
> The rich get richer every day,
> Monopolising all life's joys,
> While the poor the piper have to pay.

By the 1870s the music halls included such famous ones as Sam Collins's, the Alhambra, Gatti's and, among those in the East End, the Cambridge, which Blanchard Jerrold described as 'a handsome hall, with appointments as good as those of the halls of the West End'. Also popular were the melodrama houses, such as The Standard in Shoreditch, advertised as 'the largest and most magnificent theatre in the world.' At The Standard, real horses galloped across the stage (and out into the street outside where a policeman would hold up the traffic), or one hundred and fifty fairies were flown on wires during a ballet. Aerial effects, including flights out over the audience, as in the sensational Kellar's levitation act 'from stage to dome without mechanical aid,' were very much a feature of this period. Also popular, especially at The Standard, were nautical dramas, with small boys stirring under painted canvas to simulate waves. London in the nineteenth century was a great port: London Docks, India Docks, Victoria Docks, St Katherine's Docks, Commercial Docks, The Tobacco Dock . . . the London docks alone received something like two thousand ships a year.

Apart from The Standard, there was also the Pavilion in Whitechapel, billed as 'The Great Nautical Theatre of the Metropolis,' while Sadler's Wells had long been a favourite theatre of sailors, even becoming, for a brief period, a water theatre. This was in 1804, when a huge water tank was installed beneath the stage and the theatre opened that season with *The Siege of Gibraltar*. When the curtain rose to reveal 117 model ships sailing across the water, with the Rock of Gibraltar and its fortress in the background, the wind filling the sails, and the ships firing a salute to the audience as they passed, the audience roared with excited delight. Ships were sunk, blown up, and when 'Sir Roger Curtis saving the Spanish sailors from a watery grave' was represented with real boats in the foreground, manned 'by children for sailors picking up other children, who were instantly seen swimming and affecting to struggle with the waves, the enthusiasm of the audience exceeded all bounds.'

The music hall, however, was, above all, theatre by the people for the people. This was the secret of its greatest stars, such as Marie Lloyd and Dan Leno. When Marie Lloyd sang about booze and the bailiffs, about the ordinary events in the life of the audience, she did so from experience. The song that she first sang, and which made her famous, was addressed to the poorest in her audience:

> The boy I love is up in the gallery,
> The boy I love is looking at me.
> Where is he?—Can't you see?
> Waving his handkerchief—
> Merry as a robin
> That sings on the tree.

In the truest sense, Marie Lloyd knew how to play to the gallery.

Compared with the legitimate theatre with its melodramas and, later, the more naturalistic but nonetheless genteel comedies of Robertson, the music hall brought to London theatre a refreshing and Elizabethan note of bawdiness, of frankness, and this at a time when, it should be noted, the influence of Dr Bowdler had excised from Shakespeare all lines and words that might shock the nice sensibilities of the middle-class audiences.

With the flamboyance of Pistol, the earthiness of Mistress Overdone, and the directness of Mercutio, Marie Lloyd would hurry on stage, apologise for being late and announce, suggestively, 'Sorry I'm late. I got blocked in the Strand!' Or, frantically struggling with an umbrella, which finally opened, she would gasp and say, 'Thank God! I haven't had it up for months!' As T. S. Eliot wrote, 'It was, I think . . . the capacity for expressing the soul of the people that made Marie Lloyd unique and that made her audience . . . not so much hilarious as happy.'

One evening, while she was singing her famous ditty about a girl who 'sits among the cabbages and peas,' an outraged voice rang out from the stalls, 'Stop! Stop!' The voice was that of Mrs Ormiston Chant, self-elected chairman of the Purity Party, and an enemy of the music hall. One of her crusades, during which she crossed umbrellas with the young Winston Churchill, was to purge the Empire, the most palatial of the music halls, of the ladies who promenaded during the performances at the back of the dress circle.

These women were no ordinary prostitutes but the aristocrats of their profession. They were, as Macqueen Pope has described them, 'amazing creatures, amazingly dressed . . . they were quite unmistakable, yet their manners were excellent. They never accosted a man—there was never any loud chatter, shrieking laughter, or bad language. . . . There were all types for all tastes, from the regally majestic to the quiet and demure.' Among these ladies there were also youths, of respectable parentage, in women's clothes, as was revealed by the famous case of Ernest Boulton and Frederick William Parkes who, in 1870, had been observed entering the Strand Theatre in women's clothes. *The Times*, reporting the trial, stated 'The case excited unusual interest probably owing to the notoriety acquired by certain young men who for years past have been in the habit of visiting places of public resort in feminine attire.'

Mrs Chant succeeded in getting a screen of canvas and trellis work erected between the promenade and the bars at the Empire, in order to conceal the women of the town from the more genteel members of the audience. A crowd of two or three hundred, including the young Churchill, tore down the barricades and carried the wreckage in procession through Piccadilly. Brass railings subsequently replaced the trellis work. On 5 November 1894, Mrs Chant's effigy was burnt in place of the traditional Guy Fawkes, and her supporters (referred to by the elder statesman among critics of the day, Clement Scott, as 'Prudes on the Prowl') were defeated in the following elections. 'The music hall proprietors have a very strong ally in the public, whose opinion of the Puritan party,' wrote *The Era*, 'was expressed in no uncertain voice at the County Council elections.' Nonetheless, the fact remained that, at the turn of the century in London, the Alhambra and Empire Theatres in Leicester Square were famous not only for their spectacular international variety, but also for the fact that they provided, in the words of A. E. Wilson, 'a gilded rendezvous for the man about town and the moneyed seeker after pleasure.'

'The auditorium of a theatre,' wrote Bernard Shaw in 1909, 'with its brilliant lighting and luxurious decorations, makes an effective shelter and background for the display of fine dresses and pretty faces. Consequently theatres have been used for centuries as markets for prostitutes.'

Within a few years of the new century, the prostitutes were finally driven out of the theatres.

Chapter seven

The Nineteenth Century: III

*Punch men·pleasure gardens·exhibitions·Tom Thumb·one-man
shows·reform·intellectual theatre*

Charles Dickens's household was not alone in its love of amateur theatricals which,
along with shadow and puppet plays and tableaux vivants, were popular with
most families in the middle-class homes of Victorian London; while, outside, the
streets teemed with every kind of entertainment, from muffin men to chimney-
sweepers, lamplighters to shoeblacks, gipsies selling brushes, and the hurdy-
gurdy man with his tiny monkey in uniform. Working-class children would
follow the Punch and Judy men for miles, and Victorian children's books offer
frequent glimpses of children in middle-class homes, their noses pressed against
the nursery window-pane, waiting for their father to send out a servant with a
coin for a performance on the pavement outside. Often, on these occasions, quite a
crowd would gather and when the show was ended, the assistant would pass
round his 'bottle' for pennies, while the puppeteer hoisted his frame onto his back,
and the two would set off for another neighbourhood. 'We in general walks from
twelve to twenty miles every day, and carries the show, which weighs a good half
hundred, at the least. Arter great exertion, our woice werry often failus us, for
speaking all day through the "call" is werry trying, specially when we are
chirruping up so as to bring the children to the winders.'

   With the decline of the marionette theatres towards the end of the eighteenth
century, the Punch of the travelling showman's booth returned to the streets as a
glove puppet, and by 1825 Punch was hailed as 'the most popular performer in the
world.' In 1856 Mayhew discovered that there were about eight Punch and Judy
frames still working in London.

   'The barrel organ is the opera of the street folk and Punch is their national
comedy figure,' wrote Blanchard Jerrold in the 1860s. 'I cannot call to mind any
scene on our many journeys through London that struck the authors of this
pilgrimage more forcibly than the waking up of a dull, woebegone alley to the
sound of an organ. The women leaning out of the windows—pleasurably stirred
for an instant, in that long disease, their life—and the children trooping and
dancing round the swarthy figure.'

   'It is equalled only by the stir and bustle, and cessation of employment, which
happen when the man who carries the greasy old stage of Mr Punch halts at a

favourable "pitch", and begins to drop the green baize behind which he is to play the oftenest performed serio-comic drama in the world. The milk-woman stops on her rounds; the baker deliberately unshoulders his load; the newsboy (never at the loss for a passage of amusement on his journey) forgets that he is bearer of the "special edition"; the policeman halts on his beat—while the pipes are tuning and the wooden actors are being made ready within, and dog Toby is staring sadly round upon the mob. . . . Surely he is the very merriest fellow, the truest benefactor . . . that has ever paced the hard streets of London! . . . He is comedy, farce, and extravaganza to his audiences—Shakespeare and Molière, Morton and Planché. Many strangers with whom I have lingered over the great street comedy, have surveyed the tiers of pale faces, from the babes pushed to the front, to the working men and women in the rear, and have exclaimed that it was a terrible sight. Laughter sounded unnatural from the colourless lips. To take the cause of this smile from them because there are fastidious ears which shrink at the sharpness of the street pipes, would be a downright cruelty and shame.'

In the summer months the London Punch men would go into the country wheeling the frame in front of them, like Dickens's Codlin and Short. Travelling circuses were also popular. In 1825 Hone observed at Bartholomew Fair one which billed itself as 'Clarke from Astley's' and announced that it was 'lighted with Real Gas, In and Outside.' It was in 1815 that Lord Byron, who was on the management committee of Drury Lane, wrote 'C. Bradshow wants to light the theatre with *gas,* which may, perhaps, if the vulgar be believed, poison half the audience and all the dramatis personae.' However, the risk was taken and when it opened for the autumn season 6 September 1817, Drury Lane was lit entirely by gas. Other theatres soon followed its example. By 1840 gas had replaced candles in nearly every theatre. The introduction of gas had two important consequences affecting more than stage lighting. The first was an appalling increase in the number of theatre fires. Often a ballet dancer's muslin dress would drift against a lamp and burst into flame, burning her to death, perhaps, before the flames could be extinguished. Accounts of such deaths appeared frequently in the press. Julia McEwan, Fanny Smith, Emma Livry (the first ballerina of France) and Clara Webster (the hope of English ballet) were killed in this way. Clara, sister to Ben Webster, had been rapidly winning recognition as one of the most brilliant of the new British dancers, and a rival to the French and Italian ballerinas. On 14 December 1844, she was to dance one of her finest roles, Zelika, the slave in *The Revolt of the Harem.* The back of the stage was lit by a sunken trough of oil-burning lamps. Her flimsy dress touched one of the flames and began to burn. The other dancers recoiled from her in order to save themselves from catching fire. Her dress in flames, she rushed downstage in panic. A carpenter threw his coat over her and put out the flames but she was appallingly burned and died two days later. Ways were known to fireproof materials, to provide lamps with guards, but the most elementary precautions were not taken and there were no fire regulations obligatory upon theatre managements.

The second consequence of the introduction of gas lighting was the dimming out of the auditorium lights so that audience and actors were no longer equally lit. By 1881 electric lighting had appeared, thereby adding flexibility and safety.

Astley's Amphitheatre was the popular home of equestrian melodrams and displays. 'Dear, dear, what a place it looked, that Astley's', recalls Dickens in *The Old Curiosity Shop*, 'with all the paint and gilding and looking-glass, the vague smell of horses suggestive of coming wonders; the curtain that hid such gorgeous mysteries; the clean white sawdust of the circus; the company coming in and taking their places; the fiddlers looking carelessly up at them while they tuned their instruments, as if they didn't want the play to begin, and knew it all beforehand! What a glow was that, which burst upon them all, when that long, clear, brilliant row of lights came slowly up, and what feverish excitement when the little bell rang and the music began in earnest.'

Pleasure gardens, both in the West and East ends of London, provided a variety of *al fresco* entertainments, especially in such a heat wave as that which assailed London during the Whit holiday of 1846, when steamboats carried thousands up and down the Thames and when, in the space of eight days, no fewer than 65,000 people were said to have bathed in the Serpentine. While London's theatres (with the single exception of Tom Thumb at the Lyceum Theatre) recorded the worst business in living memory, the Vauxhall, Cremorne and Surrey Gardens were crowded. Londoners, standing on the bridge over the Thames, watched ascending balloons by day and exploding fireworks by night. 'The masses are all for out-of-door revelry,' recorded the *Illustrated London News*.

The Cremorne Gardens, a favourite resort of the young Thomas Hardy (on one occasion he even had a walk-on part at Covent Garden in *The Forty Thieves*), was a fairyland of lights, with lawns and banks of flowers sweet smelling in the dusk. In the centre stood a pagoda and, surrounding it, a dance floor for four thousand people, with a band of fifty players. There were arbours for lovers, as well as a maze in which they could escape from conscientious chaperones; side shows, firework displays, a circus, supper-rooms, and two theatres (one of which was a puppet theatre). Individual performers would also set up their turns: courting couples were often startled by a Herr von Joel, who would appear unexpectedly from the bushes, giving imitations of birdsong.

In Kensington there was Batty's Grand National Hippodrome, where 'Trojan youths and Thessalian steeds' took part in tournaments and chariot races, or ostriches were ridden by Arab boys. In 1851 an aquatic tournament took place on the Thames. For this entertainment a fortress was erected and 'attacked' by fourteen steamers. Accompanying the 'fleet' was the hulk of a derelict boat, filled with explosive, which burst into flames at the climax.

People took to the air as well. Balloon ascents were frequent, and there was always someone, like Madame Genevieve in 1861, attempting to cross the Thames on a tight-rope. Educational exhibitions were also a typical form of entertainment of the period. Vast numbers of people who were reluctant to visit the theatres because of the rough audiences looked to these exhibitions for both instruction and entertainment. There was the Chinese Collection at Hyde Park Corner which, as well as curios, included dancers and musicians and, at Easter, a special Feast of Lanterns.

In Upper Regent Street at the Polytechnic (opened in 1975 as the Regent Theatre) a scientific exhibition displayed a diving-bell within a huge glass tank, where members of the audience could be submerged and experience the pressure inside their heads. There was also a diver who sat at the bottom of the tank and to whom the bystanders threw pennies.

In Baker Street, there was Madame Tussaud herself, a tiny bespectacled old lady who had made waxworks at Versailles for Louis XVI, who sat at a table and took the entrance money for her priceless exhibition. Off Tottenham Court Road there was the Glaciarium, with a surface area of over 4,500 square feet of artificial ice, and a picturesque glacier and other painted scenery. In lecture rooms everywhere, were endless panoramas and dioramas of topographical views and battle scenes.

In 1844, there arrived from America a showman named Barnum, who hired the Egyptian Hall in Piccadilly (then currently showing an exhibition of Ojibbeway Indians from Lake Superior) and presented a miniature man, only twenty-four inches high, known as General Tom Thumb. As a result of the midget being taken up by Queen Victoria, and being announced as 'now under the patronage of H.M. The Queen,' the exhibition became the most popular entertainment in London.

That Easter the exhibitions offered a greater variety of attractions than did the theatres. At Covent Garden there were only promenade concerts, conducted with a jewelled baton—handed to him on a silver salver by a liveried footman—by the theatre's flamboyant manager, Monsieur Jullien; and at Drury Lane, light entertainment was the only bill of fare. At the Theatre Royal, in the Haymarket, James Robinson Planché presented *The Drama At Home*, a satire on the current state of London's theatre in which he depicted the Spirit of Drama being shown all the theatres of London and seeking in vain for a resting place. For the Grand Finale, Puff asks the Spirit of Drama, 'Will you receive the London exhibitions?', to which the Spirit replies 'Yes, for I'm told there are such sights to see, The town has scarcely time to think of me.' The first to enter are the Ojibbeway Indians, who are followed by Tom Thumb singing:

> Yankee Doodle went to town
> On a little pony.
> This little man of great renown
> Who struts like little Boney—

this latter a reference to Tom Thumb's appearance in the costume of Napoleon among his various turns. He is followed by Madame Tussaud, then the diver and his diving-bell from the Polytechnic, and, finally, the Chinese Collection, singing:

> Ching-a-ring-a-ring-ching! Feast of lanterns!
> What a crop of chopsticks, hongs and gongs!
> Hundred thousand Chinese crinkum-crankums
> Hung among the bells and ding-dongs!

As Raymond Fitzsimmons has described in *Barnum in London*, after taking London by storm, Tom Thumb went to Paris and, having ridden down the Champs Elysées in his open carriage, the crowds shouting 'Vive le General Tom Pouce!', returned to London, bearing gifts from King Louis Philippe, to appear for the first time on stage in a play—*Hop O' My Thumb* on 16 March 1846 at the Lyceum Theatre. The play, part of the usual long variety bill, did not commence until 9 p.m., so that Barnum was able to ensure that his protégé also continued to give three performances a day at the Egyptian hall.

In the play, Tom Thumb revealed quite a comic talent and when, at the end, he was driven off in his famous blue-and-white miniature carriage, drawn by four tiny ponies, he was called for again and again, and showered with flowers. The opening night of *Hop O' My Thumb* was the theatrical event of the month and not to have seen it was considered unfashionable. Even Macready felt compelled to fall in with his close friend Charles Dickens's suggestion that they should visit the Lyceum to see Tom Thumb.

Tom Thumb's success brought forth a rash of dwarfs, just as the success of Master Betty had resulted in a plague of child performers. As *Punch* caustically remarked, 'Tom Thumb's successes have called forth dwarfs from every nook and corner of England. England has taught human nature the exceeding advantage of being little. Hence we have had dwarfs from Germany, Spain and, very recently, dwarfs from the Highlands.'

Following Charles Foote, who had created the first one-man show in 1747, Charles Dibdin in 1791 had opened his own *Sans Souci Theatre* in the Strand, where he staged a one-man entertainment of songs and monologues, entitled *Private Theatricals*. He then moved to a second *Sans Souci* in Leicester Place in 1796, remaining there until 1804. This form of entertainment was even more successfully exploited by Charles Mathews, the comedian, who went solo in 1808. His *At Homes* were, in various forms, to last for twenty years. In 1826 Frederick Yates went solo at the Adelphi, until he linked up with Mathews. In 1833 the first woman solo performer, Frances Maria Kelly, a nineteenth-century Ruth Draper, at the Strand Subscription Theatre, offered her *Dramatic Recollections and Studies of Character*. She was followed in 1848 by Fanny Kemble, giving readings from Shakespeare. She opened at the St James's, using the versions her father had adapted for his two-hour readings at the same theatre. Preceded by a footman bearing an enormous tome which he reverently placed between two immense candlesticks upon a mahogany table placed centre stage, she would make a stately entrance, bow to the audience, and lower herself upon the high backed chair which the flunkey positioned for her. But of all the one-man shows of the nineteenth century, the readings of Charles Dickens from his own novels were probably the biggest success. From the time he was eight years old, when his family had brought him to London for a Christmas pantomime, and he had clapped his hands 'with great precocity' at Grimaldi, Dickens had been besotted with the theatre, had written plays, acted in amateur theatricals, and numbered many actors among his closest friends.

The cheers that greeted his first appearance at St Martin's Hall in 1858 could be heard streets away, and nightly the waiting carriages stretched down Long Acre to Leicester Square. 'Dickens does it capitally!' said Thomas Carlyle, 'such as *it* is, acts better than any Macready in the world: a whole tragic, comic, *theatre,* visible, performing, under one *hat!*'

The Rev. Benjamin John Armstrong, Vicar of Dereham, Norfolk, from 1850 to 1888, was a great theatregoer, and in 1859 he records going to visit another of these one-man shows. 'Went with my father to see "Woodin's carpet bag and sketch book." This Woodin impersonated upwards of fifty characters. His imitations were really admirable and the rapidity with which he changed his dress marvelous.'

Other entries from the diaries afford us valuable glimpses into some aspects of London theatre in the Victorian era.

26 January 1859
'In the evening my father took us to the famous pantomime at Drury Lane. Three of the scenes were lovely with floating fairies in the air and a cascade of real water from the top to the bottom of the stage. The children were highly delighted.

[There then follows an example of theatre-in-the-streets:] Saw an exhibition of canary birds in the street. They danced on the tight-rope, climbed up ladders, and sat in a little phaeton to which others harnessed themselves and dragged it.'
7 January 1862
'Took the children to the Alhambra to see the wondrous Leotard who, for some months, has been astonishing the world with his marvellous and elegant leaps, or rather flights, from one swing to another—he calls them 'the flying trapeze' . . . the Alhambra is something in the American free and easy style, everybody drinking, smoking and enjoying themselves. The names of the American drinks amused me—e.g. Brandy Smash, Renovator, Hail Columbia, Locomotive etc.'
21 July 1863
'In the evening took the boys to the Polytechnic to see Pepper's Ghost—a most extraordinary optical illusion of a misty transparent nature, dying out by

degrees, dissolving into thin air.' [Pepper's Ghost was a device by which a ghost could be made to appear on stage, invented by 'Professor' J. H. Pepper, a director of the Royal Polytechnic Institution, where the Ghost Illusion was first shown on 24 December 1862 and then exhibited publicly with great success. Dickens used it in connection with his readings of *The Haunted Man*. It was first used in the theatre on 6 April 1863 at The Britannia Theatre and several plays were written specially to introduce it.]

21 May 1879

'Took my younger daughter to the Westminster Aquarium where no one pays attention to the fishes on account of the admirable amusements provided, e.g. Blondin on the rope, acrobats, a comic pantomime and a lady of huge proportions who lifts tremendous heavy weights and supports on her shoulders a cannon which take four men to lift.'

29 May 1879

Took my daughter Lily to the *Opera Comique* to see H.M.S. *Pinafore* with which I was a trifle disappointed. I was confirmed in my impression as to the great lack of theatrical talent in London at this time. The 'house', however, is beautiful—a separate armchair for each person with plenty of room for your legs. It is as free and well-ordered as a theatre in Paris. The Princess of Wales and her brother, Prince Waldemar of Denmark, witnessed the performance. The ladies had bouquets in front of them as big as parasols.'

24 February 1881

'Took two of my nieces to see Corney Grain at St George's Hall. Performance really very good indeed and the place quite filled with highly respectable people, probably from the suburbs and of the class who think it wrong to go to the theatre but innocent to see theatrical representation at a hall.

12 May 1885

'Visited the Aquarium. It has degenerated into little better than a polite music hall. People were taking no interest in the tanks some of which were empty. An elephant of six years old rode a bicycle.'

In the final decades of the century, London theatres gradually developed individual identities, each actor-manager creating his, or her, own following. As society became increasingly class-conscious so also did the theatre. Complaints now appeared in the press about the presence in the pit of chimney-sweepers with soot still on them. Conduct became, as Mathew Arnold remarked, the most of life. The traditional cheapest seats in the pit now became, in some theatres, the most expensive stalls; although in most theatres they were maintained over the next seventy-five years. The theatre critic and scholar, J. C. Trewin, recalls that as a young man in the Twenties, when he was first playgoing, he invariably went in the pit, sometimes queuing most of the day. At the Court Theatre, under the management of John Hare, ices and coffee were served in the interval in place of oranges and ginger beer. In a number of theatres the pittites were relegated, or elevated, to the gallery, out of sight, if not out of hearing or out of smell.

It was in the 1870s, when F. B. Chatterton was manager of Drury Lane, that, during the fourth act of *Richard III* a hungry spectator occupying a seat in the front row of the gallery felt inclined to enjoy his supper and the performance together. 'Removing from a paper parcel the savoury nourishment he had brought with him,' described the *Illustrated London News,* 'it was his misfortune to drop a small pork pie over the gallery railing; and his shrieking ejaculation of horror and woe-begone look, as he saw the rich repast he had contemplated with such expectant delight lodge in the centre of a dress circle chandelier far below, first called the attention of the audience to the circumstances. Presently, as the pork began to frizzle in the gas-jets, a most appetising odour pervaded the house, and, a few fragments of crisp piecrust dropping through convenient apertures in the chandelier among the persons in the pit, there was an evident scramble for the succulent morsels which were devoured with manifest relish. In a short time attention became more directed to the flavoursome fumes of the frizzling pork pie, and the pursuit of the oleaginous morsels occasionally falling into the pit, than to the description of the "devouring boar" on the stage. Everybody began to feel hungry and the eager looks of the supernumeraries forming the contending armies of Richmond and Richard centred, not on their opponents on the field of Bosworth, but on the chandelier exhaling such delicious fragrance. The fun reached its height when, on a call for the manager, a wag in the pit cried out, "Mr Chatterton, is that a real Melting Mowbray pork pie?"'

Many of the pittites deserted to the music halls and were replaced by the new middle-class. The security provided by the new policemen encouraged respectable people to venture out at night, while theatres would advertise: 'The performance will always finish by eleven o'clock so as Families may be induced to support the theatre.' As the make-up of audiences changed, so did the entertainment. First, the after-piece, then the curtain-raiser, was dropped, and plays were shortened from four to three acts, and commenced later. The Bancrofts at the Prince of Wales were the first to succeed in making their middle-class audiences dine earlier in order to take their seats by 7.45 p.m.

Henry Irving's knighthood in 1895 (followed in sequence by those for Squire Bancroft, Charles Wyndham, John Hare, Beerbohm Tree, Arthur Pinero, and George Alexander) set the seal of respectability upon London's theatre. With more and more people going to the theatre, there developed a growing interest in the craft of acting. In 1883, *The Gentle-Man's Magazine* had noted, 'The revival of interest in the actor's art is perhaps the most remarkable social phenomenon.' Visits to London by such eminent actors as Salvini, Edwin Booth, Mounet-Sully, Sarah Bernhardt, and the publication of Walter Pollock's translation of Diderot's

Paradox Sur Le Comedien in 1883, and in 1888 of William Archer's *Masks and Faces, A Study in the Psychology of Acting,* all helped to generate new ideas.

But, although theatres were mushrooming, and more and more people going to them, apart from the genteel naturalism of Robertson's drawing-room comedies and the fashionable problem plays of Pinero, the drama still slumbered, unaware that a new movement was abroad, started in the 1870s by Emile Zola, and taken up by such writers as Ibsen, Chekhov and Strindberg. It is not surprising therefore to find that in 1873 Matthew Arnold was moved to say, 'We have no drama at all.'

In 1889, however, there occurred the important visit to London of the Théâtre Libre of Antoine from Paris, which caused Archer to write of their production of *La Mort du Duc D'Enghien*: 'a new departure of great moment. It is an attempt to put an historic episode on the stage in its unvarnished simplicity, without any involution of plot or analysis of motive,' and by 1890 it had become almost impossible to think of reform in the London theatre without reference to the Théâtre Libre. On 13 March 1891, at the Royalty Theatre, J. T. Grein's Independent Theatre opened with the first English production of Ibsen's *Ghosts*. In the programme, Grein pointed out how this play, banned by the censor in England, was able to be seen, read and discussed by students of the drama in Berlin, Brussels, Copenhagen and Amsterdam but 'the London theatre alone, ruled by an iron rod of medieval narrowness and dictatorship, ruled by the fear of Mrs Grundy and Sweet Fifteen, dared not produce the most modern, the most classical drama of the age.'

The battle against the censorship had begun when Walpole had passed his Licensing Act in 1737, but had been exacerbated by the Theatres Act of 1843, which held that all stage plays had to be submitted to the Lord Chamberlain, who could refuse to license a play which contained material considered to be detrimental to 'the preservation of good manners, decorum . . . or public peace.' In 1909, seventy-one writers and theatre directors, including Shaw, Wells, Galsworthy and Granville Barker, wrote to the Prime Minister, H. H. Asquith, an open letter of protest which they afterwards published in *The Times*:

'They protest against the power lodged in the hands of a single individual, who judges without public hearing, and against whose dictum there is no appeal—to cast a slur on the good name and destroy the means of livelihood of any member of honourable calling. They assert that the censorship has not been exercised in the interests of morality, but has tended to lower the dramatic tone by appearing to relieve the public of the duty of moral judgement. They ask to be freed from the menace hanging over every dramatist of having his work and the proceeds of his work destroyed at a pen's stroke by the arbitrary action of a single individual, neither responsible to Parliament nor amenable to law. They ask that their art be placed in the position enjoyed under law by every other citizen. To these ends they claim that the licensing of plays should be abolished. The public is sufficiently assured against managerial misconduct by the present yearly licensing of theatres which remains untouched by the measure of justice here demanded.'

Not until 1968 was the office of the Lord Chamberlain's Examiner of Plays formally abolished.

Although J. T. Grein's Independent Theatre was short-lived, its name and its policy and its practice made possible the emergence of a new drama and, immune from the Lord Chamberlain's censorship of publicly performed plays, the membership and club societies that began to spring up (The Stage Society was founded in 1899 to encourage new writing) enabled the presentation of avant-garde plays in the following decades. Five of Ibsen's plays were staged, and in 1896 three of London's leading actresses, Janet Achurch (the first English Nora), Elizabeth Robins (the first English Hedda) and Mrs Patrick Campbell, appeared together in four matinées of *Little Eyolf*. The passing of the Married Woman's Property Act, the founding of the National Society for women's Suffrage, and the institution of Girton and Newnham Colleges, saw the emergence of a new theatregoer, young, female, and emancipated, whose spokesman was to be Bernard Shaw, and the year 1904, with the Vedrenne–Barker season at the Royal Court Theatre, was to see the emergence of this new author and his public. The success of this season proved that there was a public for an intellectual theatre but, at the same time, that it was a limited public and therefore uneconomical unless, as Granville Barker argued, the Royal Court were to emulate the repertory system of the State-subsidized theatres of the Continent. This ideal was to become the dominant factor of London theatre in the twentieth century, giving birth to Granville Barker's long cherished dream of a National Theatre.

Chapter eight

The Twentieth Century : I

matinée idols·The Vortex·*club theatres*·Cavalcade·*Ivor
Novello*· *We Never Closed*· *The Round House*

'Early in this century,' Cecil Beaton has written, 'when the West End was lit with
gas lamps, and motor vehicles were only starting to replace the hansom cabs, when
Piccadilly was the centre of good-humoured old ladies selling wired button holes
and "sweet lovely roses" to toffs on their way to a theatre and supper (stalls at ten
and sixpence, supper at Romano's for about a guinea), London seemed to be an
entity . . . audiences were more in the nature of one large family and the leading
players and the stars became universal favourites.'

Matinées in particular became the fashionable pursuit of rich ladies who liked to
lunch with a friend and do a play together, but they went less to see the play than
their particular idol, be he George Alexander or Lewis Waller. The younger
women who, while they had no necessity to earn a living, envied those who did for
the independence it brought them (this is the theme of Barrie's one-act play, *The
Twelve-Pound Look*) always went to a thinking play. They were the supporters of the young Bernard Shaw, of John Galsworthy, and the many small
play-going societies. This minority audience of intellectuals or 'blue stockings'
was very different from those enthusiastic galleryites and pittites who formed
especial attachments to individual stars, such as the group who were known as
K.O.W.—the Keen Order of Wallerites, and who cheered, sighed, and wept at
every appearance of Lewis Waller, as similar audiences were to do, two and three
decades later, for Ivor Novello.

The images of the Edwardian matinée idols entered the homes of thousands who
never saw them in the theatre through the medium of the picture postcard. Gladys
Cooper (the greatest of the picture postcard beauties), Phyllis and Zena Dare,
Henry Ainley, Lewis Waller and hundreds more, became the pin-ups of the
Edwardian era. Perhaps the matinée idol *par excellence* was Gaby Deslys, admired
of monarchs and of J. M. Barrie, her every appearance, as Cecil Beaton recalls,
adding excitement to her myth—'The crowds waited for her at the stage door and
were never disappointed. They gasped as she appeared clad from head to foot in
magenta with a windmill of paradise feathers on her head, or dressed entirely in
black and white furs, to step into her Rolls Royce.'

Of all the names that were household words, however, as Anthony Curtis observes in *The Rise and Fall of the Matinée Idol,* that of Lily Elsie was the most popular next to that of Marie Lloyd. Lily Elsie was the personification of *The Merry Widow,* whose waltz was whistled by every errand boy and which, conducted by Franz Lehar, had taken London by storm in 1907 when it opened at Daly's, proving to be the most popular operetta of the twentieth century. Merry Widow hats were sold by the thousand, so broad that they obscured visibility in the theatre for those behind them, and so awkward that they were a hazard to the wearers getting in or out of a hansom cab.

This was a period when plays were written not merely to be staged but read— hence the witty and descriptive stage directions of James Barrie or Bernard Shaw which helped to visualize the play for the genteel reader reclining in a hammock or on her chaise-longue.

Farce and romantic drama were, in general, the fashion; heroes were handsome and heroines beautiful, yet, interestingly, beneath the surface an unexpected realism was to be found. Barrie's *The Admirable Crichton,* with its tale of role reversal, anticipates with sharp irony the break-up of the social order that was to come after 1918; while Gerald du Maurier as Captain Hook in the original production of *Peter Pan* in 1904 would have startled the more sentimental audiences of today. 'When Hook first paced his deck,' relates Daphne du Maurier, 'children were carried screaming from the stalls, and even big boys of twelve were known to reach for their mother's hand in the friendly shelter of the boxes. How he was hated . . . that ashen face, those blood red lips, the long dark greasy hair, the sardonic laugh, the maniacal scream . . . he was a tragic and rather ghastly creature who knew no peace, and whose soul was in torment; a dark shadow, a sinister dream, a bogey of fear who lives perpetually in the grey recesses of every small boy's mind.' By 1914 those twelve-year-old boys were being enlisted and the bogey of fear became a reality that slaughtered tens of thousands of young men.

During the war, musicals such as *The Bing Boys Are Here,* followed by *The Bing Girls Are Here* and, later, *The Bing Boys on Broadway, Peg O'My Heart,* and *Romance,* played to packed houses. It was a period when the control of theatres moved out of the hands of the actor-managers into those of the speculators who, lacking all knowledge of theatre, found it easy to make money out of the uncritical escapist war-time audiences. Theatres were sold and resold, let and sublet, and, though with the end of the war the boom vanished, London theatre was permanently crippled by the escalation of rents, added to which was the additional burden of the new Entertainments Tax.

In 1919 a meeting was held in Hampstead to discuss what Bernard Shaw called 'the predicament of the theatre.' Henry Arthur Jones spoke out against 'the speculative commercial manager,' while Norman MacDermott proposed to found, in a converted drill-hall, the Everyman Theatre. 'The intent was to bring back to the London stage established English authors who had been driven from the theatre by the war-time hysteria and to show that our choice of plays would be in the tradition of dramatic literature and not bedroom farce or leg show. At that time few English authors, old or new, were writing for the theatre.'

It was at the Everyman Theatre, in 1923, that there was staged a play that made its author, Nöel Coward, also its leading player, famous overnight. The London theatre of the Twenties, usually labelled escapist and trivial, produced in this play, *The Vortex,* a precocious attack by one of the 'Bright Young Things' on the values of the Twenties. 'A dustbin of a play!' shrieked *The Daily Express,* and the cry was taken up by Sir Gerald du Maurier, the doyen of the matinée idols: 'The public are asking for filth . . . the younger generation are knocking at the door of the dustbin!' A cry, ironically, that Coward himself was to echo in 1961 when he wrote a series of articles deploring 'the decline of the modern theatre' in much the same terms. Thus does the whirligig of time bring in its revenges. In 1924, however, he replied by attacking his older contemporaries for pandering 'to the desire of the British public to be amused and not enlightened . . . . Is the theatre to be a medium of expression setting forth various aspects of reality, or merely a place of relaxation, where weary business men and women can witness a pleasing spectacle, demanding no concentration?'

The Twenties were to produce other shocks if of a more ephemeral nature. 'When Mr Novello washed his legs in the first scene, 'wrote St John Ervine in 1926, reviewing *Down Hill,* a play by David L'Estrange (a pseudonym for Ivor Novello and Constance Collier), 'one heard the sound of indrawn breath from the maidens in the pit. Here was a thrilling spectacle to be described with the utmost particularity on the morrow. . . . His knees, his shins, even his thighs, and his dear little wiggly toes! If there were palpitations in the pit, there were sighs of satisfaction in the gallery.'

The galleryites and pittites continued to be vociferous judges of a play or performance, as in past centuries. In 1927, at Daly's, Ivor Novello starred in Noel Coward's play *Sirocco,* directed by Basil Dean. From the moment the curtain rose there were signs of animosity in the gallery, and at the climax of the second act when the two stars made fervent love on the floor, the scene was greeted with catcalls and loud laughter. The final curtain fell to a storm of booing. For years afterwards, as Basil Dean remarks in *Seven Ages,* the title became a synonym in theatrical circles for a disaster: one actor to another—

> 'How was it last night?'
> 'Sirocco, old boy!'

The Evening Standard wrote on the following day, 'The predominant performance of the evening was that of the gallery and it was not to the gallery's credit.'

The behaviour of the gallery, where seats were unreserved and had to be queued for, often for several hours, was a continuing subject of controversy until,

41.   Strolling players, 1834.

42.   Punch on the roads. In the summer the London Punch men would go into the country wheeling their frames in front of them, like Dickens's Codlin and Short.

43.   With the decline of the marionette theatres at the end of the eighteenth century, Punch returned to the streets as a glove puppet and by 1825 was hailed as 'the most popular performer in the world'.

44. Al fresco entertainment at the Vauxhall Gardens in the 1840s.

45. 'The general prospect of Vauxhall Gardens.'

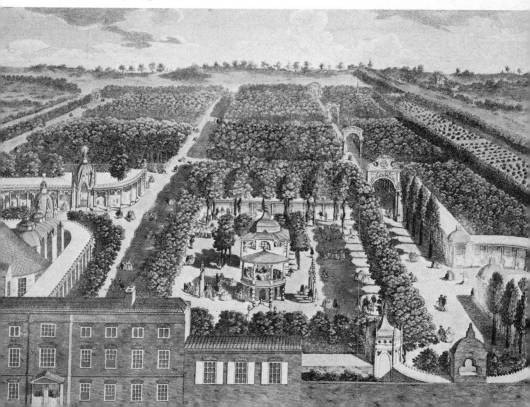

46. General Tom Thumb—a midget brought to England from America by the impresario Barnum—who took London and other capitals by storm.

47.   Dickens's last reading—of all the one-man shows of the nineteenth
century, the readings by Dickens were probably the biggest success.

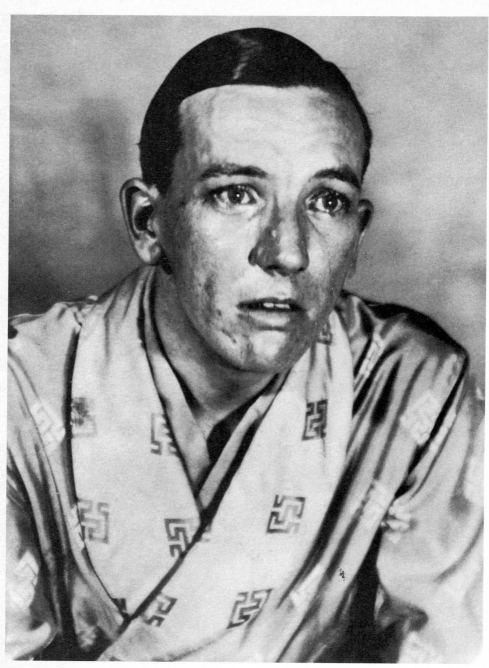

48.   Nöel Coward in *The Vortex*, which he wrote and which made him famous overnight both as an actor and playwright.

49.   Two matinée idols—(left) Lily Elsie and (right) Gaby Deslys.

NEW LINDSEY THEATRE
DIRECTION F. PIFFARD-FOXES
PRESENTS
BRITISH PREMIERE
PICK-UP
GIRL
BY ELSA SHELLEY
7TH NIGHTLY TUES-TO-SUN
MATINEES SATS-&-SUNS 3TH

51.   The famous shipwreck scene from Ivor Novello's *Glamorous Nights*.

50.   Queen Mary, an ardent patron of the theatre, after seeing *Pick-up Girl* at
the New Lindsey Club in 1946. The censor's ban was subsequently lifted on
this play and it transferred to the West End.

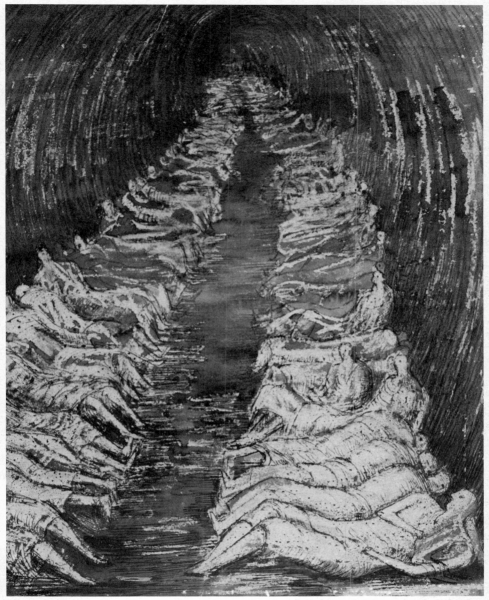

52.   *A Tilbury Shelter* by Henry Moore. As theatres closed down because of enemy bombing, many thousands of Londoners were forced to sleep underground.

53.   The Windmill Theatre, home of strip revues, which, after the Second World War, proudly proclaimed 'We Never Closed'.

54. The Royal Coburg Theatre, 1818. Gradually its middle-class audiences dwindled and it sunk into disrepute until, as the Old Vic, it became a people's theatre under the leadership of Lilian Baylis.

55. Dame Lilian Baylis, the most outstanding woman in the history of London's theatre. She succeeded in creating both a people's theatre and the embryo of a national theatre.

56.   The deeds of the first site of the National Theatre being handed over to Bernard Shaw by Sir Robert Vansittart.

57.   Sir Laurence Olivier, first director of the National Theatre, greeting Queen
Elizabeth II at a performance by the National Theatre Company in its temporary
home at the Old Vic.

58. The interior of The Olivier, one of the three auditoria of the National Theatre. It is a theatre that succeeds in combining intimacy and space, and recreates something of the physical immediacy of the Elizabethan playhouse.

in the Sixties, the increasing price of theatre seats led to all seats being bookable, and the camaraderie of the Gallery First Nighters was dissolved.

From the Twenties until the outbreak of the Second World War, the membership or club societies flourished. Norman Marshall, in *The Other Theatre*, recalls how, in 1925–6, as a young man, he saw thirteen plays of Shakespeare, Elizabethan and Restoration classics, all five of Chekhov's full-length plays, and one apiece by Molière, Ibsen, Gogol, Calderon, Andreyev, Dostoevsky, Turgenev, Hauptmann and Benavente. The contemporary dramatists included Pirandello, Cocteau, Lenormand, O'Neill, Kaiser, James Joyce, Capek, Jean-Jacques Bernard, O'Casey and Shaw, whose *Man and Superman* was given in its entirety that season. Hardly any of these plays were staged in the West End. 'The theatre which staged most of them was struggling for existence in strange out of the way places such as a drill-hall in Hampstead rechristened the Everyman Theatre; a forgotten playhouse in Hammersmith (the Lyric) which for years had been a furniture store; a cramped little cinema out at Barnes where Komisarjevsky was performing miracles of production on a tiny stage; and a backstreet attic in Floral Street, Covent Garden, in which the Gate Theatre had just been started by Peter Godfrey and Molly Veness. In the Waterloo Road the Old Vic, housing its own opera company as well as a Shakespeare company, managed to put on ten plays during the course of the season; while at King's Cross, the Euston Palace of Varieties, rechristened The Regent, had become a refuge for plays denied entrance to the West End. The rest were staged by Sunday night societies for one performance.'

In 1926 there occurred the General Strike, followed by massive unemployment that finally reached three million. The year 1929 saw the Wall Street crash and imminent national bankruptcy, leading, in 1931, to the formation of a National Government. Coincidental with the nation's traumas was the occasion of Nöel Coward's spectacular documentary at Drury Lane—*Cavalcade*, staged in October 1931, described the following year by Ashley Dukes as 'the most popular play that London has seen in ten years.' Spanning the first thirty years of the century, as seen through the eyes of one family and its servants, the production cost £30,000 to stage and employed a cast and backstage crew of over four hundred people.

'It played,' wrote Malcolm Muggeridge in *The Thirties*, 'to large and enthusiastic audiences, the *Daily Mail* serialized it, royalties came rolling in; the recent past was recalled, its most dramatic episodes—the Boer War, Mafeking, the sinking of the *Titanic*, the Great War, Armistice Day; once popular songs, still remembered, were sung, and past fashions portrayed. The days that were no more! Tears, manly and womanly, flowed in the stalls, and the pit and gallery wept like anything to see such quantities of sentiment. At the end, a glass of champagne was lifted, white dress-shirt gleaming, bare arms and back fleshly, hearts broken but bank balance intact; and a toast was drunk to England's recovered greatness, to Ramsay MacDonald, it almost seemed. He had saved the country. Money was saved, England was saved—or so it seemed at the time. The audience rose spontaneously to their feet and the National Anthem was played and sung with deep emotion. God save our gracious Pound, long live our noble Pound, God save the Pound!'

The Theatre Royal at Drury Lane remains still one of London's most imposing theatres. It is also one of the most difficult to run profitably. During the Twenties it was kept solvent by a series of American imports—*Rose Marie, The Desert Song, Show Boat*. In *Cavalcade* Coward gave it one of the greatest successes of its history, followed however (such is the way in which the theatre's pendulum so often swings), by a series of flops until, in 1935, there was staged a musical extravaganza *Glamorous Nights*,' devised, written and produced by Ivor Novello'—a gigantic Ruritanian spectacle which included a shipwreck, reminiscent of the *Titanic,* in full view of the audience.

The wreck commenced with several explosions, smoke pouring across the stage. Then, to the accompaniment of bellowed orders from the crew, fog horns blaring, and the screams of terrified women and children, the whole ship lurched to one side and began to sink. The curtain fell, and rose again on a scene of total chaos. The audience, shattered and delighted, needed the interval in which to recover. Novello followed this success with others such as *Careless Rhapsody, Crest of the Wave*, and *The Dancing Years*.

On 2 September 1939, the audience at Drury Lane for a performance of *Glamorous Nights* was so sparse, the stalls almost empty, that Novello invited people from the gallery to come down and fill up the empty seats. The evening developed into an impromptu concert. The next day war was declared.

In November 1939, Ashley Dukes, writing in *Theatre Arts*, observed: 'The soil of the National Theatre site is being excavated to fill sandbags, which is the most useful function it can now perform . . . over London the multitudinous barrage balloons hang in the dusk like extinguished lanterns. . . . The blackout falls, but it is not for ever.'

At first all theatres were closed, and even when reopened people were reluctant to go out in the blackout at night. With their audiences gone, many of the theatres closed down. Some were hit by bombs. Only the Windmill Theatre, with its mildly erotic strip-tease acts, continued to function; the theatre's proud motto was: 'We never closed', or, as the wits lisped, 'We never clothed.'

In spite of falling bombs, Myra Hess gave lunchtime recitals of piano music, and at the Strand Theatre, Donald Wolfit presented scenes from Shakespeare. The Old Vic was turned into a shelter where thousands of Londoners slept and ate their meals until, in 1941, it was severely damaged by bombs. At the little Players Theatre, offering its version of Victorian Late Night Joys, secure in its basement in Albermarle Street, the management invited customers to 'bring a rug and cushion if you wish to stay the night.'

The immediate post-war period of the late Forties saw a fresh flowering of small try-out theatres, which included the Boltons, the New Lindsey, the Embassy at Swiss Cottage, the Q at Kew Bridge (with a new play practically every Monday), and then, in the Fifties and Sixties, there came such theatres as the Hampstead Theatre Club, the Mermaid, the Shaw, the Open Space, the Questors at Ealing, Greenwich, and many more. The Sixties saw a variety of peripatetic companies, many of whom, passing through London, would be seen at the Round House (a converted, circular train-shed, built in the 1840s by Robert Stephenson as a turntable for his engines) which, in the opinion of many, including Peter Brook, is the most exciting theatre building in London. Until 1960 it had been occupied by a firm of wine merchants. The building was discovered by Arnold Wesker, who at once realized its potential as an environment for theatre, music and the arts. It was opened in 1963. Flexible in its space, friendly in its atmosphere, it has housed Peter Brook's company from Paris, the Living Theatre, the Grand Magic Circus (as well as a real circus), symphony concerts conducted by Pierre Boulez, jazz and pop concerts and children's workshops. In 1975 a smaller auditorium, the Theatre Downstairs, was opened, more suited to intimate and experimental productions. In general the movement in London theatre has been towards a more intimate relationship of audience and actors, influenced by the ideas of William Poel and, in the Fifties, of Stephen Joseph, employing the use of thrust stages, end stages and theatre-in-the-round. Thus, four hundred years after Burbage's first theatre, the movement is backwards towards the recovery, or rediscovery, of the essential qualities created by the form of the Elizabeth playhouse. The variety of London's theatre buildings, which range from upper rooms in public houses, to a theatre in a morgue (the New End Theatre Club), an inflatable dome in London's parks (the Bubble Theatre), or the redesigned Open Air Theatre in Regent's Park, and the grander, historic playhouses, is matched by a variety and richness of acting that has made London theatre an attraction for visitors from all over the world. Apart from the Round House perhaps the other most exciting theatre space in London is the Cockpit Theatre, which opened in 1970 and was then the first public London theatre to be built chiefly for drama, music and mixed media performances in the round for three hundred years; it was also the first fully flexible London theatre to have a public licence. The hub of the Cockpit is an intimate, professionally equipped theatre-in-the-round, adaptable to thrust and end staging, and subsidized by the Inner London Education Authority as a centre for young people, a research base for teachers and youth leaders exploring new creative approaches to their work, as well as for young professionals.

The post-war resurgence of theatre was signalled by the return to London of the Old Vic Company in 1944 (before the war had ended) at what was then the New Theatre (now the Albery), its home base having been damaged by bombs and not then restored. Under the joint direction of Laurence Olivier, Ralph Richardson and

John Burrell, the seasons that followed demonstrated the possibilities inherent in the concept of a National Theatre, when the very best talents available were brought together in a repertoire of great drama. These were the memorable years of Olivier's Richard III—a performance in the Kean tradition—of Richardson's Falstaff and Olivier's Justice Shallow, of Sybil Thorndike's Jocasta, of Alec Guiness's Fool and Olivier's Lear.

From 1944 to 1949 Olivier helped to run the Old Vic at the New Theatre and from 1946 onward, as he has recorded, 'it was the intention that the enterprise which had begun in the Waterloo road and moved from there to St Martin's Lane, should culminate in a National Theatre on the South Bank.' That this dream should have been realized was to Olivier a source of great pride and fulfilment when, in 1963, he was appointed the first artistic director of the National Theatre. An actor in the great tradition of Garrick, Kean and Irving, able to attract to his banner the most outstanding talent in the English theatre, he was the man most uniquely fitted to lead a great playhouse.

Chapter nine

The Twentieth Century: II

a national theatre·the Old Vic·Lilian Baylis·The National Theatre Company·the South Bank

QUEEN ELIZABETH I: Your tables begin to anger me, sir. I am not here to write your plays for you.

SHAKESPEARE: You are here to inspire them, madam. For this, among the rest, were you ordained. But the boon I crave is that you do endow a great playhouse or, if I may make bold to coin a scholarly name for it, a National Theatre, for the better instruction and gracing of your Majesty's subjects.

QUEEN ELIZABETH I: Why, sir, are there not theatres enow on Bankside and in Blackfriars?

SHAKESPEARE: Madam: these are the adventures of needy and desperate men that must, to save themselves from perishing of want, give the sillier sort of people what they best like; and what they best like, God knows, is not their own betterment and instruction. . . . Wherefore I humbly beg your Majesty to give order that a theatre be endowed out of the public revenue for the playing of those pieces of mine which no merchant will touch, seeing that his gain is so much greater with the worse than with the better. . . .

QUEEN ELIZABETH I: Master Shakespeare, I will speak of this matter to the Lord Treasurer.

SHAKESPEARE: Then am I undone, madam; for there never was yet a Lord Treasurer that could find a penny for anything over and above the necessary expenses of your government, save for a war or a salary for his own nephew.

BERNARD SHAW

It was in 1848 that a London publisher, Effingham Wilson, issued a pamphlet in which he proposed that a national theatre be created by national subscription where the works of Shakespeare might be constantly performed, at a price that would be within the reach of all, and that the Government should hold this theatre in trust for the nation. In spite of the interest aroused, no practical steps were taken, and it is significant that both Dickens and Kemble, who were generally in favour of the idea, were pessimistic about its realization.

The increasing prosperity of the commercial theatre in the second half of the nineteenth century, as well as the mushrooming of new theatres, seemed to militate against the necessity of such a theatre, while the knighthood for Henry Irving in 1895 only confirmed the general feeling that, in the Lyceum Theatre, where Irving's productions were staged, the nation already possessed a national theatre. Irving himself, however, was keenly aware of the transient nature of theatre and that no theatre of national importance could depend upon the talents of any single man. In 1878, he delivered a paper on the idea of a National Theatre in which he asked, 'Is a National Theatre desirable? Is its establishment upon a permanent basis possible? With regard to its desirability I have little, if any, doubt. In this country, artistic perfection of a high ideal is not always the road to worldly prosperity; and so long as open competition exists there will always be found persons whose aim is monetary success rather than the achievement of good works. In order that the stage may be of educational value it is necessary that those who follow its art should have an ideal standard somewhat above the average of contemporary taste. This standard should be ever in advance, so that as the taste and education of the public progress, the means for their further advancement should be ready. To effect this some security is necessary.

'As the National Theatre must compete with private enterprise . . . it should be so strong as to be able to merge in its steady gain temporary losses . . . secondly, the corporate body should be to a certain extent elastic. The production of talent in a country or an age is not always a fixed quantity . . . thirdly, the National Theatre should be independent. Once established under its proper guarantees, it should be allowed to work out its own ideas in its own way.'

In 1904, William Archer and Harley Granville Barker published privately a document entitled, *A National Theatre, Scheme and Estimate*, with an endorsement signed by Henry Irving, Squire Bancroft, J. M. Barrie, John Hare, Henry Arthur Jones, and A. W. Pinero. The bulk of the book consisted of a detailed examination of such fundamental matters as the size and character of the building, its probable cost, the theatre's constitution and government etc.

'It is essential,' wrote the authors, 'to break away completely and unequivocally from the ideas and traditions of the profit-making stage; and it is essential that the new system should have sufficient resources to give it time to establish itself and take hold upon the public. It must bulk large in the social and intellectual life of London . . . it must be visibly and unmistakably a popular institution, making a large appeal to the whole community.'

The book was issued to the general public in 1907, and as a result there was formed the Shakespeare Memorial National Theatre Committee whose objects were:

1. To keep the plays of Shakespeare in its repertory.
2. To revive whatever else is vital in the English classical drama.

3. To prevent recent plays of great merit falling into oblivion.

4. To produce new plays and to further the development of modern drama.

5. To produce translations of representative works of foreign dramatists, ancient and modern.

6. To stimulate the art of acting through the varied opportunities that it would offer to the members of the company.

An appeal was launched, and many methods were used to acquaint the public with the idea of a National Theatre, the most original of which was a one-act play, written especially for the purpose, by Bernard Shaw, entitled, *The Dark Lady of the Sonnets*. Mettings were held, adjourned, reconvened, over the years, and, after the First World War, the British Drama League, under the leadership of Geoffrey Whitworth, became its most powerful advocate. In 1930 Harley Granville Barker brought out a new book on the National Theatre, the chief and most controversial aspect of which was his insistence on the need for two theatres under one roof, not as a luxury, but as a necessary condition if the theatre was to pay its way and to use the acting company to its fullest within the repertory system.

Between 1930 and 1934 there were endless committee meetings, as various possible sites for a building were considered and rejected. Finally, in 1937, a site was discovered in Cromwell Gardens and purchased for £75,000, although it was realized that it was too small to accommodate two theatres, while Lewis Casson was doubtful if there would be sufficient storage accommodation necessary for a repertory system.

It was now decided that Granville Barker should be approached to become the director of the proposed National Theatre to be built at Cromwell Gardens but Barker, predictably, declined on the grounds that it would not have the two theatres which he considered essential.

On 23 April 1938 the handing over of the title deeds of the site to the Shakespeare Memorial National Theatre Committee took the form of a simple ceremony at which Shaw made a speech. 'People sometimes asked him,' he said, 'Do the English people want a National Theatre?' Of course they did not. They never wanted anything. They had got the British Museum, the National Gallery, and Westminster Abbey, but they never wanted them. But once these things stood as mysterious phenomena that had come to them they were quite proud of them and felt that the place would be incomplete without them.

The whole project, however—and in the long run, fortunately—was brought to a halt by the outbreak of the Second World War. It was in March 1942 that the next development took place, when the Shakespeare Memorial National Theatre Committee was approached by the London County Council and invited to put forward plans for a new theatre on the South Bank which, taking advantage of the larger area of land available (between Westminster and Waterloo Bridge), would include the two theatres envisioned by Granville Barker. In the winter of

1944 there took place, behind the scenes, another meeting of major importance, when Geoffrey Whitworth was sent for by Sir Reginald Towe, the Honorary Treasurer of the Old Vic, and told that the Old Vic had been considering amalgamation with the National Theatre. The idea that the National Theatre Committee should be associated with an existing company such as the Old Vic, which could provide the nucleus of a national theatre company, appealed very strongly and the way was now prepared for a Royal Charter of amalgamation once a national theatre building had been erected.

In the eighteenth and nineteenth centuries, Covent Garden and Drury Lane were the main homes of great acting in the London theatre. Towards the end of the nineteenth century the Lyceum, under Irving, took their place. But in the twentieth century another London theatre, the Old Vic, takes pride of place. The Royal Coburg, founded in 1818, under the patronage of Princess Charlotte and Prince Leopold of Saxe-Coburg, was at first a theatre for those who lived in the rural area around Waterloo. In 1824 its chandeliered auditorium was reflected in a looking-glass curtain, which became one of the sights of London. Here, in 1831, the great Edmund Kean acted at a fee of £50 a performance (the price paid to a top courtesan in 1762, so Boswell informs us—also for a single performance). In 1833 the theatre was renamed the Royal Victoria after the new Queen.

As the slums of London spread, and the middle-classes moved further out to the suburbs, so the neighbourhood declined and the theatre in the Waterloo Road, where Vestris had danced, Paganini had played the violin, Macready and Kean and Aldridge had acted, became a rowdy music hall, 'a licensed pit of darkness' as Charles Kingsley described it.

In 1880, Emma Cons, a social reformer, whose prime concern was the betterment of the working-classes in the under-privileged areas of London, took control, assisted by Samuel Morley, M.P. for Bristol, and began to transform it into a 'cheap and decent place of amusement on strict temperance lines,' renaming it 'The Royal Victoria Hall and Coffee Tavern.' The sale of liquor on the premises was stopped, and she began to include in the weekly variety bill concerts of music, lectures and classes and, in 1900, the first operatic production, *The Bohemian Girl*. In due course, out of all this activity was to emerge Morley College, the Royal Opera and the Royal Ballet.

It was in 1898 that Emma Cons was joined in this work by her niece, Lilian Baylis, who in 1912, on the death of her aunt, took over the running of the Old Vic and turned it into a home for Shakespeare, making it, in effect, the first working National Theatre. It became, and remained, the true successor to Phelps's Sadler's Wells. From 1914 to 1923 all Shakespeare's plays were presented for the first time in the First Folio text.

Lilian Baylis has become one of the legendary figures of the British theatre. She believed that the theatre is 'our greatest power for good or evil' and 'a crying need for working men and women.' She ran her theatre with an eccentric and missionary zeal and, caring nothing for fame, helped to make it one of the most important theatres in the world, and the best-loved theatre in London. She was present at almost every performance, seated in her box, its red curtains drawn across, doing her accounts, answering letters, frying sausages, ready at any moment to poke out her head to see how the audience were enjoying the play. Regularly she addressed them from the stage—'And look here, you bounders, Monday nights have got to be better!'

The Old Vic, during the First World War and after, was rapidly established as a theatre with a purpose and a public, offering opportunities to young actors and actresses and directors, even though overworked and underpaid. Once again, as in the days of the Surrey melodramas, and the first Elizabethan playhouses, audiences began to cross the river, to see the plays of Shakespeare, while over 1700 school-children arrived weekly at the matinées.

'My first appreciation of Shakespeare,' recalls Malcolm Muggeridge, 'came a little later when I attended a series of special matinées for school-children at the Old Vic, at which we saw most of the better known plays. We paid sixpence for our seats, and fourpence for the journey by train from Croydon to Waterloo; swaying and screeching our way through Streatham and Brixton on those old double-decker LCC trams whose connections with overhead electric cables on frosty days gave off clouds of sparks. I dare say the Old Vic productions were pretty rough and the scenery scanty—I seem to recall mostly curtains—but I loved every minute of them. The star was Sybil Thorndike, who seemed to take almost every part, male and female, though she can't have played Lear; I remember her brother in the role, memorable because at one of the most dramatic moments his beard came off.'

This was during the First World War, when the number of available men was very small. Dame Sybil Thorndike recalled that 'on the first night of *King Lear* Waterloo Station was bombed. We carried on with the performance under the racket of gunfire and the dropping bombs, and just as Russell [Thorndike] reached the splendid speech beginning "Blow winds and crack your cheeks! Rage! Blow!" there was a tremendous explosion outside the theatre and the whole building shook. Russell strode downstage with me at his heels—I was playing the Fool— and shook his fist at the roof and shouted "Crack Nature's moulds, all GERMANS spill at once!" The cheers of the audience almost drowned the sound of the guns!'

After the First World War, Shakespeare in London leaned more and more heavily upon the Old Vic. Between 1920 and 1925 Robert Atkins, a disciple of William Poel, did more for Shakespeare in the theatre than anybody of his generation. He was followed, in turn, as director at the Old Vic by Andrew Leigh and Harcourt Williams. Following the example of Granville Barker, the plays were staged simply, leaving the actors to demonstrate that the play was the thing. The verse was no longer ponderously declaimed but spoken swiftly and incisively. Ernest Milton, John Gielgud, Edith Evans, Ralph Richardson, were among the many actors who established themselves at the Old Vic as the rising new actors of the London theatre in the twentieth century.

In 1931 Lilian Baylis also took over the derelict Sadler's Wells, raised money to have it rebuilt, and began to alternate productions of opera and Shakespeare between the two theatres. 'We were never able to remember which of the two theatres we were supposed to be acting or rehearsing in,' wrote John Gielgud in *Early Stages*. 'No sooner did we begin to play to good business in one than we were transferred to the other where the audience promptly dwindled.' In the end, Lilian Baylis chose to concentrate on Shakespeare at the Old Vic, and opera and ballet at Sadler's Wells.

In 1937 she died and Tyrone Guthrie was appointed director. With the outbreak of the Second World War the company left London. In 1950 the Old Vic was reopened and became once more the home of Shakespeare, presenting between 1953 and 1958, when Michael Benthall was in charge, all the plays in the Shakespeare canon, in the First Folio text, the only exception being the non-Folio *Pericles*.

In 1949 the National Theatre Bill was passed by both Houses of Parliament without a division. A Building Committee under the joint chairmanship of Sir Laurence Olivier and Norman Marshall was set up, and an architect, Denys Lasdun, appointed to design the new theatre on the South Bank. Sir Laurence Olivier was appointed the first director of the National Theatre and in 1963 the Old Vic finally became the temporary home of the newly formed National Theatre Company.

In 1960, at the age of twenty nine, Peter Hall had formed, from the seasonal company at Stratford-upon-Avon, a permanent ensemble. Joined later by Peter Brook and Michel Saint-Denis he took at the end of that year the Aldwych Theatre in London as a base for the company, where, in addition to Shakespeare, the company could also stage productions of contemporary plays by such authors as Harold Pinter, Edward Albee, David Mercer, as well as revivals of other plays, both English and European.

In 1973 Peter Hall succeeded Lord Olivier as artistic director of the National Theatre and in 1976 the National Theatre Company moved from the Old Vic to its new home on the South Bank, adjacent to the Royal Festival Hall, the Queen Elizabeth Hall, the Purcell Room, the Hayward Art Gallery and the National Film Theatre.

The new National Theatre comprises three theatres (instead of Granville Barker's original two): the Cottesloe, a small rectangular space with adjustable seating capable of holding up to 400 people and intended for experimental work by the National Theatre Company and by visiting fringe groups; the Lyttelton, a proscenium theatre seating 890: and the Olivier, a theatre with an open stage and an auditorium, seating 1,160, related to it like a fan.

In 1944 James Agate had written, 'One of my more horrid nightmares is about a national theatre. I envisage a gaunt hideous building, half barracks, half public baths, stuck down in a part of London remote from restaurants, and unfriendly in approach.' As Denys Lasdun's concrete building began to arise, tier by tier, terrace by terrace, there were many who thought that Agate's dream had come true. But, in the event, its reception was on the whole enthusiastic. 'Well, it works,' wrote Michael Billington in *The Guardian* on 12 March 1976, a few days after its opening. 'After all the sniping and griping, it is a relief to be able to report that the new National Theatre feels not like a white elephant or cultural mausoleum: more like a superb piece of sculpture inside which it is possible to watch a play or walk and talk in the lobbies without feeling dwarfed by one's surroundings ... architecturally, Denys Lasdun's success is that throughout he counterpoints austerity and comfort; ribbed concrete surfaces in auditorium and lobbies are off-set by soft plum-coloured carpets and muted brown seating. But, above all, there is space to move and breathe.'

The lofty and spacious interior of the foyers, as of some cathedral, is segmented by lines at different angles: vertical pillars in varying formation, horizontal terraces and bridges, diagonal ramps, curving staircases. Thus people are seen moving at different levels and distances. The building is constantly full of surprises and always there are unexpected glimpses of the river, through tall narrow slits of glass, long horizontal windows or, climbing a staircase, a low squat window, set at floor level, provides a dramatic view of the Thames far below.

Apart from productions in each of the three main theatres, the building is open day and night, with free shows, concerts and exhibitions in the foyers, bars that keep pub hours, a running buffet, while its book-stall not only sells British newspapers but copies of the *New York Times, Paris Soir* and other journals.

'We wanted a theatre,' said Bernard Shaw in 1938, 'which refused to give people merely what they wanted. There was needed some institution to give the public the best until they learned to like it. I want the State theatre to be what St Paul's and Westminster Abbey are to religion—something to show what the thing can be at its best.'

Postscript

TOUCHSTONE: Wast ever at the Court, shepherd?
CORIN: No, truly.
TOUCHSTONE: Then thou art damn'd.

AS YOU LIKE IT

The fashions of theatres rise and fall, just as new theatre buildings rise to replace those that have gone to join 'the lost theatres of London.' The story of London theatre is richer and more complex than can be contained within the pages of this book but one factor begins to emerge, as the twentieth century draws to its close: the importance of the small or chamber theatre. The Royal Court Theatre in Sloane Square, first under Vedrenne–Barker from 1904 to 1907, and then, in 1956 when, under George Devine, it became the home of the English Stage Company, has provided a nursery of talent and been a laboratory for new ideas and new methods. Its influence is out of all proportion to the actual numbers that the theatre itself can seat.

Although the small club or membership theatre—what Norman Marshall has called 'the other theatre'—took its origin from the existence of the censor and, in consequence, from the 1890s to the 1960s, consistently championed the new and avant-garde; its function then, and increasingly now, goes deeper. In the 1890s William Archer argued the case for the establishment of a cadre of little theatres in London which would cater for the discriminating minority alone—'Plays for which there is no effective demand, which are radical, unfitted for the stage and gain nothing by representation, may be very good literature, but do not belong to the living drama. What class of modern work, then, would the non-commercial theatre welcome and foster? Why, plays that appeal to the thousands not to the tens of thousands; plays that interest intelligent people without being sensational, or amusing, or sentimental, or vulgar, to run for 250 nights; plays in which the female interest is weak; plays that end, and must end, unhappily; plays, in fine, that do not fulfil all the thousand and one trivial conditions on which popular success is supposed to depend.'

As Shaw remarked at a dinner in honour of J. T. Grein, 'I believe, as Wagner said, that "music is kept alive not by the grand operas in the capitals but on cottage pianos." The theatre in England is being kept going still by a large number of small ventures—remarkabley like Mr Grein's small original venture.'

In 1933, Ashley Dukes, the founder of the Mercury Theatre at Notting Hill Gate, which pioneered the cause of poetic drama in this century with plays by T. S. Eliot, Ronald Duncan, Christopher Fry, W. H. Auden and Christopher Isherwood, and provided a home for the Ballet Rambert, asked whether 'there are any good plays (Reinhardt spectacular pieces excepted) that would not be better for being played in a theatre of half the general size. Shakespeare certainly is no exception; and the first modern producer to mount his plays in a house of Elizabethan proportions may easily make a fortune. If audiences have any Shakespearean taste today it is a desire to listen and hear every word . . . notwithstanding the work of William Poel we have no such playhouse in Britain, and nothing approaching it in construction except the Madder-market Theatre in Norwich.'

The idea of presenting Shakespeare in an intimate, chamber setting is one that preoccupies the director, Jonathan Miller, who argues the case for 'a Protestant Reformation in theatre . . . small, intense, local congregations all over England, where actors perform for no more than a hundred people at a time'. In such theatres the emphasis is upon the actor. As Granville Barker, a close friend and admirer of Jacques Copeau, once said to the latter of his work at the Vieux-Colombier, 'The art of theatre is the art of acting, first, last and all the time. You very soon found that out.'

Some theatres belong to a community; others create a sense of community; and, as the centre of London increasingly moves outwards, there are those who, like the theatre critic, Michael Billington, believe that 'instead of campaigning for the preservation of Shaftesbury Avenue we should all be better employed seeking the theatrical colonization of the London boroughs where people actually live. We already have Greenwich Theatre, the Hampstead Theatre Club, the Theatre Royal Stratford, the Albany at Deptford, as well as valued commercial outposts like Richmond and Wimbledon—and personally I would like to see a whole network of varied, vigorous, suburban playhouses, each of which took their character from the area in which they were set. I believe we should concentrate on restoring London theatre to Londoners and answering a definite community need.'

Bibliography

The following are the books that have most helped me in writing this book. 'Beauty being preferable to scholarship'—especially for the ordinary reader—to quote Anthony Burgess, I have avoided disfiguring the text with footnotes, and thus stifled the courtesy of particular acknowledgments. However, I have learned so much in the process of writing this book that I should like to record my especial debt to the following:

Chapter one

Brown, I., *Shakespeare and the Actors,* Bodley Head 1970.
Halliday, F. E., *Shakespeare in his Age,* Duckworth 1965.
Hodges, C. W., *Shakespeare and the Players,* Bell 1970.
—, *The Globe Restored,* Ernest Benn 1953.
Hurstfield, J., *The Elizabethan Nation,* B.B.C. 1964.
Norman, C., 'London Environs,' in *Theatre Arts,* April 1939.
Ordish, T. F., *Early London Theatres,* republished by White Lion Publications 1950.
Trewin, J. C., *Shakespeare on the English Stage 1900–1964,* Barrie and Rockcliffe 1964.
Wickham, G., *Early English Stages.* Routledge and Kegan Paul 1963.

Chapter two

Baker, R., *Drag,* Triton 1968.
Pepy's Diary, Macmillan 1924.
Trease, G., *Samuel Pepys,* Thames & Hudson 1972.

Chapter three

Rosenfeld, S., *Theatre of London Fairs,* Society of Theatre Research 1975.

Chapter four

Arundel, D., *The Story of Sadler's Wells,* Hamish Hamilton 1965.
Boswell, J., *London Theatre,* Heinemann 1952.
Dunbar, J., *Peg Woffington,* Heinemann 1968.
Davies, T., *Memoirs of the Life of David Garrick,* London 1780.
Bell, G., *Evelyn's Diary,* 4 Volumes, London 1904.
Findlater, R., *The Player King,* Weidenfeld & Nicolson 1971.
George, D. M., *London Life in the Eighteenth Century,* Knopf Inc. 1960.
Kelly, J. A., *German Visitors to the English Theatres in the 18th Century,* Princeton 1936.
Laver, J., *Drama—Its Costume and Decor,* Studio Books 1951.
Malcolm, J. P., *Anecdotes of the Manners and Customs of London during the 18th Century* . . . London 1810.

Mare, M. L., & Quarrel, W. H., Translation of letters and diaries describing *Lichtenberg's Visits to England*, Press 1938.

Memoirs of Richard Cumberland, London 1806.

Memories of Tate Wilkinson, York 1790.

Morley, H., *Journal of a London Playgoer*, London 1891.

Nicoll, A., *A History of the Late 18th Century Drama 1750–1800*, Cambridge 1927.

Pedicord, H. W., *The Theatrical Public in the time of Garrick*, King's Crown Press, Columbia University 1954.

Scott, W. S., *The Georgian Theatre*, London 1946.

Tenebaum, S., *The Incredible Beau Brummell*, South Brunswick and New York, A S Barnes 1967.

Chapter five

Boettcher, H., *Young Roscius*, Theatre Arts 1935.

Murray, C., *Elliston, Manager*, Society for Theatre Research 1975.

Playfair, G., *The Prodigy (Master Betty)*, Secker & Warburg 1967.

Puckler-Muskau, H. *Tour in England, Ireland & France*, London 1832.

Tait, S., 'Theatre Riots', in *Theatre Arts*, February 1940.

Chapter six

Allen, S. S., *Samuel Phelps and Sadler's Wells Theatre*, Wesleyan University Press 1971.

Dickens, C., Ed., *Memoirs of Joseph Grimaldo*, with Foreword by Richard Findlater, Macgibbon and Kee 1968.

Disher, M. W., *Blood and Thunder*, F. Muller 1949.

Downer, A., *The Eminent Tragedian, William Charles Macready*, Harvard University Press 1966.

Duncan, B., *The St. James's Theatre*, Barrie & Rockcliffe 1964.

Elsom, J., *Erotic Theatre*, Secker & Warburg 1973.

Farson, D., *Marie Lloyd and the Music Hall*, Tom Stacy 1972.

Haddon, A., *The Story of the Music Hall*, London 1935.

Hudson, L., *The English Stage*, Harrap 1951.

Isaacs, E. J. R., *The Negro in the American Theatre*, Theatre Arts Inc. 1947.

Larkin, S., 'Charles Kean, Pedant and Showman' in *Theatre Arts*, December 1934.

Mayer, D., III, *Harlequin in His Element*, Harvard University Press 1969.

Pemberton, T. E., *John Hare, Comedian*, Routledge & Sons 1895.

Southern, R., *The Victorian Theatre, A Pictorial Survey*, David and Charles 1970.

Trewin, J. C., *The Pomping Folk*, Dent 1968.

—, *Mr Macready*, George Harrap 1955.

—, *The Journal of William Charles Macready*, Longmans 1967.

Webster, M., *The Same Only Different*, Gollancz 1969.

Chapter seven

Armstrong, B., *Norfolk Diary*, Hodder & Stoughton 1963.

Avery, G., *Victorian People*, Collins 1970.

Brown, I., *Dickens and his Time*, Nelson 1963.

Delgade, A., *Victorian Entertainment*, David & Charles 1971.

Fitzgerald, P., *Memories of Charles Dickens*, Arrowsmith 1913.

Fitzsimons, R., *The Charles Dickens Show*, Bles 1970.

—, *Barnum in London*, Bles 1969.

House, H., *The Dickens World,* Oxford University Press 1960.
Hudson, L., *The English Stage*, Harrap 1951.
Mander, R., and Mitchenson, J., *Revue*, Peter Davies 1971.
Mayhew, H., *London Labour and the London Poor*, London 1851.
Planché, J. R., *Recollections and Reflections,* Sampson Low & Marston 1901.
Rowell, G., *The Victorian Theatre*, Oxford University Press 1956.
Stokes, J., *Resistible Theatres*, Elek Books 1972.
Southern, R., *The Victorian Theatre, A Pictorial Survey,* David and Charles 1970.
Webster, M., *The Same Only Different*, Gollancz 1969.
Wroth, W., *Cremorne and the Later London Gardens*, London 1907.

Chapter eight

Billington, M., *Our Theatres in the Sixties*, Hutchinson 1971.
Brown, J. R., *Effective Theatre*, Heinemann 1969.
Curtis, A., Ed., *The Rise and Fall of the Matinée Idol,* Weidenfeld & Nicolson 1974.
Dean, B., *Seven Ages,* Hutchinson 1970.
Donaldson, F., *The Actor Managers,* Weidenfeld and Nicolson 1970.
Jenkins, A., *The Twenties*, Heinemann 1974.
Macdermott, N., *Everymania*, Society for Theatre Research 1975.
Marshall, N., *The Other Theatre*, John Lehman 1947.
Muggeridge, M., *The Thirties*, Collins 1940.
Wilson, S., *Ivor Novello*, Michael Joseph 1975.

Chapter nine

Whitworth, J., The Making of a National Theatre, Faber 1975.

General reference

Colby, A., *Shakespearean Players and Performances*, New York 1953.
Dobbs, B., *Drury Lane*, Cassell 1972.
Doran, Dr, *Their Majestie's Servants—annals of the English stage,* London 1887.
Joseph, S., *The Story of the Playhouse,* Barrie and Rockcliffe 1963.
Mander, R., and Mitchenson, J., *The Lost Theatres of London,* Rupert Hart Davis 1968.
May, R., *A Companion to the Theatre,* Lutterworth 1973.
McKechnie, S., *Popular Entertainment through the Ages*, Sampson Low and Marston 1932.
Nicoll, A., *The Development of the Theatre*, London 1927.
Pope, M., *The Haymarket*, W. H. Allen 1948.
Sherson, E., *London's lost Theatres*, Bodley Head 1925.
Speaight, G., *Punch and Judy,* Studio Vista 1970.
Thaler, A., *From Shakespeare to Sheridan*, Cambridge Mass. 1922.
Young, G. M., *Early Victorian England, 1833–74*, Eyre and Spottiswood 1969.

Index

Numbers in *italic* refer to the illustrations and their captions